D0904944

PORNOGRAPHY
The Conflict over Sexually Explicit Materials in the United States

GARLAND REFERENCE LIBRARY
OF SOCIAL SCIENCE
(VOL. 64)

PORNOGRAPHY
The Conflict over Sexually Explicit Materials in the United States
An Annotated Bibliography

Greg Byerly
Rick Rubin

GARLAND PUBLISHING, INC. • NEW YORK & LONDON
1980

Library of Congress Cataloging in Publication Data

Byerly, Greg, 1949–
    Pornography, the conflict over sexually explicit
materials in the United States.

    (Garland reference library of social science ;
v. 64)
    Includes indexes.
    1. Pornography—Social aspects—United States—
Bibliography.   2. Pornography—United States—
Psychological aspects—Bibliography.   3. Porno-
graphy—Moral and religious aspects—Bibliography.
4. Obscenity (Law)—United States.   I. Rubin,
Rick, 1949–   joint author.   II. Title.
Z7164.P84B93   [HQ471]   016.3634′7   80-14336
ISBN 0-8240-9514-6

Printed on acid-free, 250-year-life paper
Manufactured in the United States of America

CONTENTS

v

INTRODUCTION

The conflict over the availability of pornographic materials in the United States has generated a significant number of books, government documents and journal articles. This conflict shows no signs of abating, and will probably continue for years to come. The need to exercise bibliographic control of the published materials on this controversy is manifest.

This book is a selective, annotated bibliography on pornography, encompassing psychological, sociological, religious, philosophical, legal and popular perspectives. Limited to works primarily concerned with the creation, availability, dissemination and effects of sexually explicit materials in the United States, it includes monographs, dissertations, government documents and journal articles in English. Chapters on pornography from books of a broader scope are not included. Emphasis is on works published in the last ten years, although some significant monographs and dissertations published in the 1960s have been included.

Items chosen for annotation had, first, to illuminate the contemporary controversy over sexually explicit materials in the United States. Second, they had to be accessible, useful research tools. Except for dissertations, unpublished materials, e.g., conference papers, are not included. Similarly, materials not generally available in the United States are excluded.

Deciding where the debate over sexually explicit materials ends and the debate over sexual politics or sexual behavior begins is extremely difficult. Related items that fall outside the bibliography's scope include:

1. works that are predominantly historical, such as H. Montgomery Hyde's *A History of Pornography* (New York: Farrar, Straus & Giroux, 1964) or Steven Marcus' *The Other Victorians* (New York: Basic, 1966);

2. works that are primarily discussions of contemporary sexual behavior, attitudes or mores. Books like Kate Millett's *Sexual Politics* (Garden City, N.Y.: Doubleday, 1970), Alfred Kinsey's *Sexual Behavior in the Human Male* (Philadelphia: W. B. Saunders, 1948) or Susan Brownmiller's *Against Our Will: Men, Women and Rape* (New York: Simon & Schuster, 1975) are not found in this bibliography;

3. works on art censorship or on censorship in general. For example, Jane Clapp's *Art Censorship: A Chronology of Proscribed and Prescribed Art* (Metuchen, N.J.: Scarecrow, 1972) is not included;

4. works that concern themselves mainly with literary criticism of pornographic works, such as Angela Carter's *The Sadeian Woman and the Ideology of Pornography* (New York: Pantheon, 1978) or Michael Perkins' *The Secret Record: Modern Erotic Literature* (New York: William Morrow, 1977);

5. works that are themselves pornographic.

Once the bibliographic citation for an article was located in such indexes as *Psychological Abstracts*, *Sociological Abstracts* and *Index to Legal Periodicals*, items were personally examined by the compilers. Monographs were located through such compilations as the annual editions of *Books in Print* and the *NUC: Books, Subject*. *Comprehensive Dissertations Index* was used to locate dissertations and as a source for abstracts of dissertations unavailable for inspection. The volume and year of the *Dissertation Abstracts International* volume used follow in parentheses at the end of each summarized abstract. The principal source for major government documents was the *Monthly Catalog of United States Government Publications*.

The book is divided into eight chapters. Chapter I includes significant monographs and dissertations published since 1960. The next five chapters list journal articles of the last ten years from psychological, sociological, philosophical, religious, popular and legal periodicals. One chapter each deals with relevant government documents and court cases. A brief summary is given for each court case included, along with official citations and references to discussions of the case.

All entries are descriptively annotated; books and major articles are annotated at greater length. Reviews are also listed, where possible, for books, and each entry includes standard bibliographic information (author, title, place of publication, publisher, dates and pages). Anonymous entries are listed alphabetically by title. Inclusion of illustrations or bibliographies is indicated. Entries are indexed by author and by subject and personal name. There is also a list of periodicals cited.

One area of special emphasis is the reports of the President's Commission on Obscenity and Pornography. This multivolume set contains many significant reports and studies that are not reproduced or indexed elsewhere. The *Report of the Commission on Obscenity and Pornography* and sixty-eight separate technical reports produced by the Commission are separately listed and annotated.

Our purpose in this book is to provide a sharply focused, accessible annotated bibliography for a broad range of researchers including teachers, librarians, students and interested laymen who are seeking information about the conflict over pornography in the United States. It should enable researchers to quickly and efficiently survey the broad range of items published on this topic and to avoid the repetition of duplicated entries in various indexes.

PORNOGRAPHY
The Conflict over Sexually Explicit Materials in the United States

I

BOOKS AND DISSERTATIONS

1. Bahm, Robert M. "The Influence of Non-sexual Cues, Sexual Explicitness and Sex Guilt on Female's Erotic Response to Literature." Ph.D. dissertation, University of Massachusetts, 1972. 111pp.

   288 female undergraduates were exposed to erotic and nonerotic stories. Results included: (1) female's arousal is not dependent on explicitness of the sexual depiction; (2) sex guilt had little effect on degree of arousal; (3) ratings as to pleasantness of material correlated with sex guilt; and (4) arousal is a result of the presence of overt sexual cues. (*DAI* XXXIII [1973])

2. Barber, D.F. *Pornography and Society*. London: Charles Skilton, Ltd., 1972. 192pp.

   Provides a general summary of the arguments and issues raised concerning the censorship of pornographic materials. Historical and social perspectives on obscenity law are explored, and an attempt is made to expose the difficulty in defining pornography. Concludes that pornography cannot be eliminated, because it is grounded in man's sexual instinct, and that censorship is an attempt to suppress our realizations of our sexuality. Feels that censorship usurps what is essentially an individual responsibility to make decisions. Includes bibliography.

3. Bosmajian, Haig A., ed. *Obscenity and Freedom of Expression*. New York: Burt Franklin, 1976. 348pp.

   Presents the decisions in numerous court cases from 1868 to 1973. Deals not only with written materials but also with drama, political speeches, broadcasting and obscenity in education. Provides judicial dissents as well as majority opinions. Includes an appendix listing obscenity statutes in other countries. A bibliography and an extensive index are also included. (REVIEWS: *Choice*, April 1977, p. 186; *Library Journal*, December 1, 1976, p. 2504)

3a. Chandos, John, ed. *"To Deprave and Corrupt ... ": Original Studies in the Nature and Definition of "Obscenity."* London: Souvenir Press, 1962. 207pp.

Contains nine essays which consider the conflict over obscenity and censorship from various points of view. Ernest van den Haag offers arguments for censorship while Walter Allen and the editor present more liberal views. Most of the essays provide historical background for the opinions argued. (REVIEWS: *Library Journal*, September 15, 1962, p. 3022; *New Statesman*, July 13, 1962, p. 50; *Times Literary Supplement*, July 6, 1962, p. 495)

4.   Cline, Victor B., ed. *Where Do You Draw the Line?* Provo, Utah: Brigham Young University Press, 1974. 365pp.

Considers two areas of contemporary concern: pornography and media violence. The conflict between freedom of speech and censorship is discussed in three essays, as are the current obscenity laws. The effects of pornography and violence in the media are presented with references to appropriate studies and research. Four essays discuss the question: "Where Do You Draw the Line?" Opinions differ, but all agree that any limit placed on free expression should represent the "consensus of a majority of our citizenry." Includes index. (REVIEWS: *Choice*, March 1975, p. 63; *Christian Century*, September 15, 1974, p. 890; *Kirkus Reviews*, August 1, 1974, p. 843)

5.√ Clor, Harry M. *Obscenity and Public Morality: Censorship in a Liberal Society.* Chicago: University of Chicago, 1969. 315pp.

Explores the contemporary controversy surrounding the censorship of obscene materials. Issues under discussion include the limits of the First Amendment and the right of a society to establish moral baselines; the character of obscenity and how it is defined; and the concept of literary value and how it relates to contemporary community standards. Argues that some censorship is permissible and offers two approaches to judging whether a work is obscene: first, assessing a work by determining if its obscene properties outweigh its "redeeming" properties as defined by the author, and second, if obscene and redeeming properties are equal, assessing the work on the basis of contemporary community standards. Suggests additional legislation for

the protection of children and against pandering. Includes notes and index. (REVIEWS: *Annals of the American
Academy of Political and Social Science*, January 1970,
p. 218; *Quarterly Journal of Speech*, December 1970, p.
450)

6. Clor, Harry M., ed. *Censorship and Freedom of Expression:
   Essays on Obscenity and the Law*. Chicago: Rand McNally,
   1971. 175pp.

   Consists of eight articles by leading figures in the
   pornography and censorship debate. The position for re-
   sponsible censorship is represented in part by Harry Clor
   and Richard Kuhn, who assert: (1) that a balance must be
   struck between the aesthetic seriousness of a work and the
   degree to which it appeals to the prurient interest; (2)
   that statutes are particularly appropriate in regulating
   access to children; and (3) that obscenity dehumanizes
   sexuality and human beings. The anticensorship position
   is represented by Richard Hettlinger, Charles Rembar and
   Willard Gaylin, who assert: (1) that censorship is arbi-
   trary and based solely on sexual themes; (2) that censorship inhibits human growth and maturity; and (3) that
   there is great danger in censoring obscenity, because it
   seriously affects the free exchange of ideas. No index.
   (REVIEWS: *Choice*, May 1972, p. 402; *Journal of Politics*,
   November 1972, p. 1319)

7. Cotham, Perry C. *Obscenity, Pornography and Censorship*.
   Grand Rapids: Baker Book House, 1973. 206pp.

   Contends that in moral terms pornography is an evil.
   Reviews contemporary examples of pornography found in
   motion pictures, the theater, television and the print
   media. From the Christian perspective pornography is
   offensive because it: (1) intrudes upon privacy and indi-
   viduality; (2) represents the antithesis of Christian
   ideals; (3) degrades and dishonors human dignity; and (4)
   has a harmful effect on society. Pornography is defined
   to include not only hard-core materials, but also less
   obvious examples of sexual permissiveness, which are labeled
   "pious pornography." No index. Questions for discussion
   included at the end of each chapter.

8. Daily, Jay E. *The Anatomy of Censorship*. New York: Marcel
   Dekker, 1973. 401pp.

   Examines the history of censorship and the attitudes of
   censors toward various types of materials. Argues that

censorship is socially undesirable and that intellectual
freedom dictates our responsibility to prevent regulation
of materials by the state. (REVIEWS: *Choice*, March 1974,
p. 70; *Library Journal*, May 1, 1974, p. 1278; *Library
Quarterly*, July 1974, p. 285)

9. Dearn, Edmund Lawrence. *Pornography Degrades*. Sydney,
    Australia: Renda Publications, 1974. 82pp.

    Compares attempts by America, Australia and New Zealand
    to deal with pornography. All base their approach on
    British law, and the reliance on criminal trials to regu-
    late pornography has proven ineffective. Pornography is
    not a "victimless crime," because it has injurious effects
    not only on those involved in producing it and those who
    consume it, but also on society at large. Concludes that
    there is a real need to control pornography so that citi-
    zens can enjoy true freedom.

9a. Dhavan, Rajeev, and Christie Davies, eds. *Censorship and
    Obscenity*. Totowa, New Jersey: Rowman and Littlefield,
    1978. 187pp.

    Collection of essays which present arguments on both sides
    of the controversy over obscenity and its control. At-
    tempts to answer three questions: (1) who censors and why?;
    (2) how do censorship laws work?; and (3) what are the ef-
    fects of censoring or not censoring obscenity? Includes
    essays by Berl Kutschinsky, John Trevelyan and Hans J.
    Eysenck. Includes list of cases and index.

10. Drakeford, John W., and Jack Hamm. *Pornography: The Sexual
    Mirage*. Nashville: Thomas Nelson Inc., 1973. 189pp.

    Argues the general thesis that pornography is a threat
    to social values because it dehumanizes and depersonalizes
    love and sexuality. Discusses the intrusion of the media
    on American life and contends that the media have distorted
    and mythologized sex. Particularly singles out movies and
    the inappropriateness of programs for family viewing.
    Recommends courses of action for those who wish to end the
    rise of pornography. These actions include: (1) inspecting
    stores disseminating such materials; (2) writing to news-
    paper editors; (3) monitoring movies and television programs;
    (4) providing a positive view of sex through sound sex
    education programs; (5) mustering public support; and (6)
    using legal channels. Includes notes. Illustrations by
    Hamm.

11. Dutcher, Linda W. "Scarcity and Erotica: An Examination
    of Commodity Theory Dynamics." Ph.D. dissertation,
    Southern Illinois University, 1975. 106pp.

    Examines commodity theory as it relates to pornographic
    materials. Theory predicts that scarcity of erotica
    should increase demand. Dutcher measured the effects of
    uniqueness deprivation, self-dissatisfaction and sex
    guilt on preferences for viewing scarce and available
    sexual and neutral videotapes in 75 students. None of
    the variables accounted for variation in choices, though
    sex of subject and sex guilt did correlate with choice
    of sexual versus neutral tapes. (*DAI* XXXVII [1976])

12. Ernst, Morris L., and Alan U. Schwartz. *Censorship: The
    Search for the Obscene*. New York: Macmillan Co., 1964.
    288pp.

    Presents a factual and historical account of censorship.
    Outlines the major laws and court cases which have formu-
    lated American obscenity law. Lengthy excerpts from famous
    judicial opinions are included and interpreted. (REVIEWS:
    Library Journal, June 1, 1964, p. 2321; *New York Times
    Book Review*, September 13, 1964, p. 10; *Saturday Review*,
    August 22, 1964, p. 27)

12a. Eysenck, Hans J., and D.K.B. Nias. *Sex, Violence and the
    Media*. London: Maurice Temple Smith, 1978. 306pp.

    Concerned primarily with television and cinema, the
    work examines the potential influence of pornographic and
    violent materials on viewers. Critically analyzes the
    findings of the Commission on Obscenity and Pornography
    and discusses various recent field and laboratory experi-
    ments assessing behavioral effects of viewing sexual and
    violent materials. Concludes, in part, that pornography
    does have its effect on viewers and that some of these
    effects are harmful. Includes index and bibliography.
    (REVIEWS: *Library Journal*, December 1, 1978, p. 2415;
    New Statesman, August 25, 1978, p. 248)

13. Frank, John P., and Robert F. Hogan. *Obscenity, the Law,
    and the English Teacher*. Champaign, Illinois: National
    Council of Teachers of English, 1966. 61pp.

    Includes two papers relevant to teachers trying to
    assess the controversy over pornography. Provides a
    general discussion of the definitional problems surround-
    ing the concept of obscenity and examines the variations
    among "experts" as to what is obscene and what is not.

Argues there are many questions, such as the relation of
exposure to antisocial behavior, that remain unanswered.
Hogan contends that most of the claims of antipornography
advocates are unfounded and that the general discomfort
over moral changes in society leads censors to choose
books as targets. Recommends that teachers take public
action to protect books, and provide students, particularly adolescents, with material that responds to their
maturation process. (REVIEW: *English Journal*, April
1967, p. 634)

14. Friedman, Leon, ed. *Obscenity: The Complete Oral Argu-
    ments Before the Supreme Court in the Major Obscenity
    Cases*. New York: Chelsea House, 1970. 342pp.

    Presents the arguments and decisions of the major ob-
    scenity cases from *Roth* v. *United States* to *Stanley* v.
    Georgia. Disagreements among justices rendering decisions
    are included. Includes index and lists of defense and
    prosecution attorneys. (REVIEW: *Kirkus Reviews*, October
    15, 1970, p. 1185)

15. Gallagher, Neil. *How to Stop the Porno Plague*. Minne-
    apolis: Bethany Fellowship, Inc., 1977. 252pp.

    Argues against pornography from a Christian point of
    view. Spiritual, civic and legal strategies are detailed
    to fight pornography. Numerous examples are cited to
    demonstrate the harmful effects of exposure to pornography.
    The author claims *Playboy* "opened the door for savage sex.
    This book closes it." Arguments against pornography are
    bolstered by biblical references. Christians are urged
    to actively fight pornography and obscenity. No index.

16. Gerber, Albert B. *Sex, Pornography, and Justice*. New
    York: Lyle Stuart Inc., 1965. 349pp.

    Analyzes the obscenity issue from a variety of perspec-
    tives. Sections relate to judicial tests for obscenity;
    theories underlying obscenity law; selected media, such
    as movies, night club acts and private letters; Supreme
    Court cases and historical roots of obscenity law. Se-
    lected passages from controversial literary works are
    provided at length along with limited photographic exam-
    ples. Argues that obscenity is indefinable, highly sub-
    jective and lacking in judicial clarity. Includes foot-
    notes, bibliography, table of cases and index. (REVIEWS:
    Antiquarian Bookman, December 1965, p. 2389; *Choice*,
    June 1966, p. 302)

17. Gerhard, Paul. *Pornography in Fine Art from Ancient Times Up to the Present.* Los Angeles: Elysium, Inc., 1969. 187pp.

    Surveys erotic art, mostly drawings, from a historical perspective. Presents examples of erotic or pornographic art not easily found elsewhere. Emphasizes the impossibility of drawing a distinction between good/legal pornographic art and bad/illegal art. Early periods in Greece, the Roman Empire, Japan and Europe are briefly covered, but the major emphasis is on contemporary pornographic art. Argues against any legal restrictions on access to pornographic art. Primarily black and white illustrations with some accompanying text.

18. Ginzburg, Ralph. *An Unhurried View of Erotica.* New York: Helmsman Press, 1958. 128pp.

    An informal and highly selective review of erotic tales and literature in England and other countries. Passages from early literature are provided along with some narrative by Ginzburg. Concludes with some observations about the contemporary erotic book market, and a list of 100 titles. Includes index.

19. Goldstein, Michael J., and Harold S. Kant. *Pornography and Sexual Deviance: A Report of the Legal and Behavioral Institute, Beverly Hills, California.* Berkeley: University of California Press, 1973. 194pp.

    The possible relationship between exposure to pornography and the development of antisocial sexual behavior is investigated. Four groups of subjects were studied: (1) extensive users of pornography; (2) convicted sex offenders; (3) homosexuals, lesbians and transsexuals; and (4) a control group from the general population. Intensive questionnaires and interviews were employed, and the results are reported in detail. No definitive conclusions are drawn, and further research is urged. (REVIEWS: *Best Sellers*, March 1, 1974, p. 332; *Kirkus Reviews*, September 1, 1973, p. 1004; *Library Journal*, November 15, 1973, p. 3363)

20. Grazia, Edward de. *Censorship Landmarks.* New York: R.R. Bowker, 1969. 657pp.

    Reproduces opinions from major obscenity and censorship cases. Includes state and federal decisions, as well as Supreme Court cases. Arranged chronologically; covers 1663-1968. Major emphasis is on cases from 1850 to 1968.

Detailed subject index and a table of cases are included.
(REVIEWS: *Catholic Library World*, October 1970, p. 129;
Library Journal, February 15, 1970, p. 642; *Wilson Library
Bulletin*, January 1970, p. 563)

21.   Haight, Anne L., and Chandler B. Grannis. *Banned Books,
       387 B.C. to 1978 A.D.* 4th edition. New York: R.R.
       Bowker, 1978. 196pp.

       Reports examples of banned books and attempted book
       bannings. Entries are listed chronologically by the
       birth dates of the authors and are briefly annotated.
       Coverage is worldwide, but emphasis is on contemporary
       American examples. Lengthy appendices include: (1) trends
       in censorship; (2) statements on freedom of the press; (3)
       excerpts from important court decisions; (4) excerpts from
       the *Report of the Commission on Obscenity and Pornography*;
       and (5) selected U.S. laws and regulations. Includes
       bibliography and index. (REVIEWS: *Library Journal*,
       December 1, 1978, p. 2407; *New York Times Book Review*,
       December 17, 1978, p. 16)

22.   Halpern, James W. "Projection: A Test of Psychoanalytic
       and Cognitive Dissonance Hypothesis." Ph.D. disserta-
       tion, New School for Social Research, 1974. 96pp.

       College students were rated as to their sexual defensive-
       ness on the Sexual Defensiveness Scale (SDS) and then
       individually exposed to pornographic materials. Results
       indicated that subjects rated as highly sexually defensive
       projected repressed sexual impulses onto an unfavorable
       other, confirming in part the classical projection theory of
       Freud. However, evidence for the cognitive dissonance
       hypothesis was inconclusive. (*DAI* XXXVI [1975]).

23.   Hart, Harold, ed. *Censorship for and Against*. New York:
       Hart Publishing Company, Inc., 1971. 255pp.

       Collection of 12 essays on the topic of censorship.
       Both sides are represented. Authors include Hollis Alpert,
       Judith Crist, Charles H. Keating, Jr., Eugene McCarthy
       and Max Lerner. All agree that censorship is a subjective
       judgment, but differ in their analyses of its efficacy and
       propriety. Index included. (REVIEWS: *Choice*, February
       1972, p. 836; *Library Journal*, September 1971, p. 2784;
       RQ, Winter 1971, p. 175)

24.   Holbrook, David, ed. *The Case Against Pornography*. New
       York: The Library Press, 1973. 294pp.

Collection of essays arguing that pornography is harmful and must be suppressed. The psychological, social and cultural aspects of pornography are considered. The political problems of controlling pornography are also described, and several essays deal with the issue of sex education. Central idea is that pornography threatens love and tenderness and results in a "hatred of man." Pornography is not simply a social issue, but also an educational and philosophical one. No index. No bibliography. (REVIEWS: *Booklist*, September 1, 1973, p. 6; *Choice*, February 1974, p. 1852; *Kirkus Reviews*, January 1, 1973, p. 38; *Library Journal*, August 1973, p. 2322)

25. Houston, Judith A. "Capturing Policies of Pornographic Pictorial Representations by Normative Judgment Analysis." Ph.D. dissertation, University of Northern Colorado, 1974.

    Explores the usefulness of the Judgment Analysis Technique (JAN) in determining definitions of pornography as perceived by a sample of lawyers, police officers and graduate students in psychology. Individuals were exposed to 150 profiles scored on 11 dimensions. Results indicated that a clear definition of pornography is a complex problem, but the JAN technique is helpful in clarifying the points of variance in individual concepts of what is pornographic. (*DAI* XXXIV [1974])

26. Hoyt, Olga G., and Edwin P. Hoyt. *Censorship in America*. New York: Seabury Press, 1970. 127pp.

    Examines the evolution of censorship in America as it relates to obscene materials. Covers the development of controversial literature in the pre-World War II period and the related changes in state laws and court decisions. Contemporary analysis is provided through discussion of obscenity in television, radio, movies and theater as well as remarks on modern court cases such as that of *Lady Chatterley's Lover*. Argues that censorship is a threat to the free dissemination of ideas, and that censorship has always failed in its purpose. Includes bibliography and index. (REVIEWS: *Kirkus Reviews*, November 1, 1970, p. 1204; *Library Journal*, December 15, 1970, p. 4326 and p. 4364)

27. Hughes, Douglas A., ed. *Perspectives on Pornography*. New York: St. Martin's Press, 1970. 223pp.

    Explores viewpoints on pornography by reprinting 14 articles by well-known literary and philosophical figures.

Included are works by Anthony Burgess, Paul Goodman,
George Elliot, George Steiner, Ernest van den Haag and
Susan Sontag. Deals with two basic questions: (1) What
are the psychological effects of erotica? and (2) Can
pornography be viewed as a form of literature? Elliot,
Stein and van den Haag serve as the primary exponents of
censoring and represent the viewpoint that erotica serves
unduly to violate human privacy, impoverishes the language,
constitutes a form of nihilism, and dehumanizes the society. Sontag, Goodman and others argue that censorship
is unwise and misguided, that pornography maintains an
aesthetic potential and dimension, and that legal action
tends to exacerbate the impoverished quality of the material. Indexed. (REVIEWS: *Booklist*, September 1, 1970,
p. 7; *Library Journal*, June 15, 1970, p. 2262; *Times
Literary Supplement*, November 6, 1970, p. 1298).

28. Hutchinson, Earl Ray. "Henry Miller and *Tropic of Cancer*,
    from Paris to Wisconsin--On the Censorship Trial."
    Ph.D. dissertation, University of Wisconsin, 1966.
    646pp.

    Deals primarily with the attempts to censor Miller's
Tropic of Cancer, focusing on the trial of the author in
Milwaukee. Discusses the political ramifications in
Wisconsin following the trial and the failure of the local
newspaper to defend illegal censorship. Argues that parents
must control access to erotica, and that the public must
learn to distinguish works of literary value from works
of no value. (*DAI* XXVIII [1967])

29. Jeffries, John Allison. "Legal Censorship of Obscene
    Publications: Search for a Censoring Standard." Ph.D.
    dissertation, Indiana University, 1968. 200pp.

    Discussion and analysis of the censorship of obscene
materials. Provides historical background tracing the
concept of censorship from the Old Testament to the contemporary controversies facing our legal and judicial
systems. Argues that the harm generated by pornographic
materials is not significant enough to warrant the legal
punishments presently employed. (*DAI* XXX [1969])

30. Kilpatrick, James J. *The Smut Peddlers*. New York:
    Doubleday and Company, 1960. Reprint, Westport,
    Connecticut: Greenwood Press, 1973. 323pp.

    Presents the arguments for and against censorship of
pornography. Outlines the decisions of the courts involving the First and Fourteenth Amendments. *Roth* v. *United*

States is discussed in detail. Agrees with the opinions
of J. Edgar Hoover and other law enforcement officials
who believe pornography incites sexual crimes. Concludes
that an effort must be made to deal with this problem,
but advocates neither censorship nor total freedom of
expression. Index and table of cases. (REVIEWS: *Kirkus
Reviews*, September 1, 1960, p. 810; *Library Journal*,
December 15, 1960, p. 4482; *New York Times Book Review*,
November 20, 1960, p. 28)

31. Kirkpatrick, Robert George. "The Socio-Sexual Dialectics
of Decency Crusades." Ph.D. dissertation, University
of Texas at Austin, 1971. 391pp.

    Studies the development of two antipornography crusades
    in two cities. The natural history of each crusade is
    analyzed, and individual traits of the participants are
    studied. Employs analytical techniques of Neil J. Smelser
    when dealing with the natural history of such crusades.
    (*DAI* XXXIII [1972])

32. Kronhausen, Eberhard, and Phyllis Kronhausen. *Pornography
    and the Law: The Psychology of Erotic Realism and Pornog-
    raphy*. New York: Ballantine Books, 1959. 317pp.

    Attempts to distinguish between hard-core pornography
    and erotic realism. Numerous historical examples, with
    excerpts, are provided. Supreme Court guidelines and the
    concept of "contemporary community standards" are dis-
    cussed. Two books are studied in detail: *Memoirs of
    Hecate County* and *Lady Chatterley's Lover*. The psycho-
    logical effects of erotic literature are also presented.
    Concludes that there is no workable legal definition of
    obscenity, but that erotic realism must be protected from
    censorship. Index and bibliography included.

33. Kuh, Richard H. *Foolish Figleaves? Pornography In--and
    Out of--Court*. New York: The Macmillan Company, 1967.
    368pp.

    Studies the legal and historical events involved in the
    writing, sale and possession of pornographic materials
    in the United States, and makes recommendations based on
    this analysis. Includes: (1) a detailed analysis of im-
    portant court cases including *Roth*, *Jacobellis*, *Ginzburg*
    and *Mishkin*; (2) descriptions of various types of erotica
    including girlie magazines, live entertainment, photographs,
    unusual sexual activities and sophisticated erotica; and
    (3) recommendations on the legislative level to curb the

availability of materials to young adults and in public
areas. Sample acts are provided with appropriate definitions. Notes and index. (REVIEWS: *Book World*, February
18, 1968, p. 5; *Booklist*, January 15, 1968, p. 567; *Library
Journal*, December 15, 1967, p. 4518; *New York Times Book
Review*, December 10, 1967, p. 6)

34.   Leach, Michael. *I Know It When I See It.* Philadelphia:
      The Westminster Press, 1975. 153pp.

      Defines pornography existentially as a "frontier phenom-
      enon," i.e. a specific type of material considered wrong
      by a specific culture during a certain time period. His-
      torically considers both sex and violence in the movies.
      Predicts the eventual end of pornography because sex has
      become so explicit in movies and foresees a larger contro-
      versy over violence in films. Religion and culture are
      both becoming more tolerant of healthy sexual behavior.
      Censorship is not advocated. No index. (REVIEWS: *Christian
      Century*, June 2, 1976, p. 545; *Choice*, October 1976, p.
      966; *Library Journal*, January 15, 1976, p. 359)

35.   Lewis, Felice Flanery. *Literature, Obscenity, and Law.*
      Carbondale and Edwardsville: Southern Illinois Univer-
      sity, 1976. 297pp.

      Discusses the legal and social issues in the history of
      obscenity law as it relates to literary works read in
      America. Begins with remarks on erotic material in 17th-,
      18th- and 19th-century America. Analyzes the effect of
      war and changing mores in the 20th century and examines
      the conflicts over such works as *Ulysses*, *An American
      Tragedy*, *Lady Chatterley's Lover* and *Tropic of Cancer*.
      Concludes by discussing the development of obscenity law
      in cases decided by Warren and Burger courts. Includes
      notes and index. (REVIEWS: *Booklist*, September 15, 1976,
      p. 102; *Best Sellers*, September 1976, p. 205; *Kirkus
      Reviews*, April 1, 1976, p. 445; *Library Journal*, July
      1976, p. 1546)

36.   Liston, Robert A. *The Right to Know; Censorship in America.*
      New York: Franklin Watts, Inc., 1973. 150pp.

      Attempts to rationally consider two opposing ideas: (1)
      censorship and (2) total freedom of expression and in-
      formation. Part I deals with censorship of obscenity,
      and censorship of information is discussed in Part II.
      Historical background is provided for both topics. Argu-
      ments are presented both for and against censorship, but
      censorship is concluded to be worse than the evils it

attempts to control. (REVIEWS: *Booklist*, October 15, 1973, p. 222; *Best Sellers*, September 15, 1973, p. 280; *Library Journal*, October 15, 1973, p. 3157)

37. Michael, Judy L. "A Test of Arousal Response Predictions Derived from Ego Psychology." Ph.D. dissertation, Kent State University, 1976. 71pp.

Tests the hypothesis, according to Ego Psychology, that excessive stimulation leads to struggling or distancing from the stimulation. Subjects were preselected on Byrne's Repression-Sensitization Scale and exposed individually to a pornographic movie. A female confederate was also present and reacted to the movie. Skin responses and self-reports were used as measures. Results indicated that subjects responded by approaching or struggling with the stimuli. (*DAI* XXXVII [1976])

38. Michelson, Peter. *The Aesthetics of Pornography*. New York: Herder and Herder, 1971. 247pp.

Deals with both historical and recent writings that have been considered pornographic. Argues that pornography is most productively viewed as the "literature of sexuality," and as such must be understood as an art form. Analysis includes viewing pornography as a form of poetry or poetics, as moral rhetoric or anarchy, as tragedy, and as "comic catharsis." Contends that movements to censor such materials are a denial of one's own humanity and can only be injurious to the culture. Includes index. (REVIEWS: *Best Sellers*, October 15, 1971, p. 326; *New York Times Book Review*, May 2, 1971, p. 30; *Publishers Weekly*, February 8, 1971, p. 73; *Saturday Review*, July 17, 1971, p. 33)

39. Mishan, E.J. *Making the World Safe for Pornography and Other Intellectual Fashions*. London: Alcove Press, 1973. 262pp.

Includes eight essays, some previously published, on a wide variety of topics; all attack the "Established En-lightenment" and the "permissive revolution." The title essay on pornography argues that pornography is definitely harmful to society and that laws should be used to control it. Another essay, "The Economics of Sex Pollution," also urges more controls on pornography. (REVIEWS: *Kirkus Reviews*, September 1, 1973, p. 1013; *Observer*, November 18, 1973, p. 38)

39a. Moroz, George Anton II. "Prolegomenon to an Aesthetician's
     View of 'Erotic-Art,' 'Obscenity,' and 'Pornography.'"
     Ph.D. dissertation, University of Illinois at Chicago
     Circle, 1979. 371pp.

     Attempts to clarify the meanings of the following terms:
     "erotic," "erotic-art," "obscene," "obscene-art," "pornog-
     raphy" and "pornographic." Historical definitions are
     considered, and then each set of terms is analyzed. Ob-
     scenity is judged usually by its offensiveness to certain
     human sensibilities. Concludes that "pornography" has
     primarily a negative, evaluative connotation. A detailed
     redefinition of "pornography" is presented and is con-
     trasted with the opinions of Drs. Phyllis and Eberhard
     Kronhausen. (*DAI* XL [1979])

40. Oboler, Eli M. *The Fear of the Word: Censorship and Sex.*
     Metuchen, New Jersey: Scarecrow Press, Inc., 1974.
     362pp.

     Approaches the issue of control of pornographic materials
     from the perspective of the censor. The historical, cul-
     tural and religious underpinnings of censorship are ex-
     plored with special attention paid to the Judeo-Christian
     influence. The motivation of the contemporary censor is
     explored; comments from censors such as Charles Keating,
     Jr. are provided. (REVIEWS: *American Libraries*, December
     1974, p. 612; *Choice*, April 1975, p. 203; *Library Journal*,
     February 15, 1975, p. 403)

41. Paer, William E. "Punishment and Reward Seekers in Activ-
     ities Associated with Voyeurism (Scoptophilia) and Ex-
     hibitionism." Ph.D. dissertation, United States Inter-
     national University, 1975. 130pp.

     Subjects, previously grouped into categories of punish-
     ment seekers and reward seekers, were exposed to 18 pic-
     tures, 7 of which were pornographic. GSR reactions were
     recorded. Results indicate that sexual arousal to visual
     stimuli may be universal, but punishment seekers are more
     sensitive to visual stimuli of all types. (*DAI* XXXVI
     [1975])

42. Peckham, Morse. *Art and Pornography: An Experiment in
     Explanation.* New York: Basic Books, Inc., 1969. 306pp.

     Explores the rationale behind pornography and analyzes
     its function in society. Finds many fallacies in court
     decisions dealing with pornography. The scope is much
     broader than art and pornography. Personal examples are

interspersed with discussions of linguistics, philosophy,
sociology and psychology. Contends that pornography is
essential to man's creative impulses and has played a
part in the development of Western culture. (REVIEWS:
Criticism, Fall 1970, p. 350; *Library Journal*, February
1, 1970, p. 508; *Nation*, March 2, 1970, p. 245)

43. *Pornography: The Longford Report.* London: Coronet Books,
     1972. 520pp.

Counters many of the recommendations and observations
of the President's Commission on Obscenity and Pornography.
Composed of prominent English men and women, and chaired by
Lord Longford, the committee reported on a wide variety of
subjects including: (1) violence and pornography; (2)
pornography and antisocial behavior; (3) pornography in
cinema and theater; (4) sex education; (5) broadcasting;
and (6) legal problems. Concludes that pornography has
adverse effects on the population and that more restrictive
laws should be legislated and enforced against producers.
Advocates the stimulus of public opinion to motivate legis-
lators and law enforcement personnel to act against the
dissemination of erotica. Includes bibliography and index.
(REVIEWS: *Observer*, September 24, 1972, p. 36; *Times
Literary Supplement*, September 22, 1972, p. 1083)

44. Rembar, Charles. *The End of Obscenity.* New York: Random
     House, 1968. 528pp.

Attempts to develop through court cases an understanding
of the judicial concept of obscenity and the nature of
the judicial process which defines it. Discusses in detail
the trials involving the prosecution of *Lady Chatterley's
Lover*, *Tropic of Cancer* and *Fanny Hill*. Parts of the trial
transcripts are included along with the rulings of the
judges. Concludes that obscenity as regards written literature is at an end in the courts, and that a new generation
of youth no longer finds the same excitement in the literature. Includes appendix and index. (REVIEWS: *Kirkus
Reviews*, March 15, 1968, p. 378; *Christian Century*, June
12, 1968, p. 789; *New York Times Book Review*, June 23,
1968, p. 1)

45. Ringel, William E. *Obscenity Law Today.* Jamaica, New
     York: Gould Publications, 1970. 245pp.

Examines in detail the pertinent court cases which have
elucidated and sometimes confused the concept of obscenity.
Written primarily for legal professionals and scholars,

the book reviews cases involving nudity, the written word,
newspapers, theaters and films. Analyzes the relationship of the Fourth and Fourteenth Amendments to obscenity with particular attention to the First Amendment
interpretations regarding freedom of speech. Appendix
includes representative obscenity rulings and biblio-
graphical listings. Also has a detailed table of cases.

46. Rist, Ray C., ed. *The Pornography Controversy: Changing
     Moral Standards in American Life*. New Brunswick, New
     Jersey: Transaction Books, 1975. 279pp.

     Approaches the issue of pornography from two perspec-
     tives: the philosophical and the pragmatic. 14 articles
     by prominent figures in the field are provided, including
     two excerpts from the President's Commission on Obscenity
     and Pornography. Theoretical aspects of pornography are
     discussed in relation to morality, law and aesthetics.
     Social science articles deal, in part, with effects of
     exposure to erotica. Broader articles on the social,
     cultural and definitional dilemmas of the pornography
     controversy comprise the majority of articles and include
     works by George Steiner, Peter Michelson, John Gagnon,
     William Simon and Earl Warren, Jr. Includes index and
     bibliography. (REVIEWS: *Choice*, September 1975, p. 824;
     Contemporary Sociology, January 1976, p. 32)

47. Robertus, Patricia Elizabeth. "Postal Control of Obscene
     Literature, 1942-1957." Ph.D. dissertation, University
     of Washington, 1974. 218pp.

     A historical analysis of the activities of the U.S.
     Post Office in dealing with obscene materials from 1942
     to 1957. Discusses the three major techniques used to
     avoid dissemination of such materials by the Post Office.
     These are: (1) nonmailability; (2) limitations on 2nd-
     class mailing privileges; and (3) mail blocks. Argues
     that the Post Office has acted as a censor despite the
     constitutional guarantees ensuring freedom of expression.
     (*DAI* XXXVI [1975])

48. Rushdoony, Rovsas John. *The Politics of Pornography*.
     New Rochelle, New York: Arlington House, 1974. 163pp.

     Argues that pornography is a symptom of much larger
     social and moral problems. Religious arguments are pre-
     sented against pornography. Death of God theology is
     related to the availability of pornographic materials.
     The new pornography is inspired by the Marquis de Sade

and his anti-Christian beliefs. Concludes, however, that
pornographers will be stopped by a new Christian "moral
elite." An appendix discusses various legislative approaches against pornography. Brief index. (REVIEWS:
Kirkus Reviews, July 1, 1974, p. 728; *Publishers Weekly*,
June 24, 1974, p. 59)

49. Schauer, Frederick F. *The Law of Obscenity*. Washington,
     D.C.: Bureau of National Affairs, Inc., 1976. 459pp.

     Designs an analysis of the obscenity problem specifically
     for legal professionals involved in the litigation of
     obscenity cases. Examination includes: (1) historical
     overview of obscenity law; (2) social and psychological
     aspects, including remarks on the President's Commission
     on Obscenity and Pornography; (3) discussion of the crucial
     definitions in cases, such as "average person," "prurient
     interest" and "contemporary community standards"; (4)
     discussion of state and federal regulations; and (5) jury
     selection and use of expert witnesses. Argues that ob-
     scenity cases occupy a "discreet body of law" which must
     be dealt with on a professional level. Takes no position
     on the general desirability of such laws. Includes ap-
     pendices of pertinent statutes and court cases, a topical
     index and table of cases cited.

50. Schroeder, Theodore. *"Obscene" Literature and Constitu-
     tional Law*. New York: Theodore Schroeder, 1911. Re-
     print, New York: Da Capo Press, 1972. 439pp.

     Basic early work on obscenity and the law. Main con-
     tention is that censorship of obscene materials is un-
     justified because obscenity is judged subjectively, not
     objectively. Explores the historical relationship between
     obscenity and freedom of speech. The conflict between
     prosecuting obscenity cases and guaranteeing due process
     is also discussed. Obscenity laws are unconstitutional
     because they violate the First Amendment and are typi-
     cally very vague and undefinable. Index and table of law
     cases. (REVIEW: *AB Bookman's Weekly*, November 27, 1972,
     p. 1684)

51. See, Carolyn. *Blue Money*. New York: David McKay Company,
     Inc., 1974. 234pp.

     Explores the various aspects of the pornography industry
     and discusses selected individuals who have played signi-
     ficant roles in its growth and popularity. Provides anec-
     dotal accounts of her interviews and contacts with such
     notables as Marvin Miller, Matt Cimber, Linda Lovelace,

Jim Holland and Burton Marks. Other topics include notes
on live sex shows and a discussion of two participants, and
an analysis of antipornography organizations, focusing on
the Legion of Decency. No index. (REVIEWS: *Booklist*,
September 1, 1974, p. 8; *Kirkus Reviews*, May 1, 1974,
p. 527; *Library Journal*, August 1974, p. 1972; *Publishers
Weekly*, May 20, 1974, p. 62)

52.   Sharp, Donald B., ed. *Commentaries on Obscenity*. Metuchen,
      New Jersey: Scarecrow, 1970. 333pp.

      Anthology of commentaries designed for the lawyer or
      scholarly layman dealing with the legal and constitutional
      issues surrounding obscenity rulings. Inspired by the
      recent and somewhat contradictory court decisions of the
      1960s, authors develop historical perspectives and cite
      specific opinions that elucidate the divisions and con-
      ceptual difficulties in obscenity law. Specific atten-
      tion is given to the Ginzburg case and its possible rami-
      fications for the freedom to read. Includes notes and
      index.

52a. Simons, G. *Pornography Without Prejudice: A Reply to
      Objectors*. London: Abelard-Schuman, 1972. 169pp.

      Examines various definitions of pornography and analyzes
      the main arguments presented by antipornographers. Con-
      tends that pornography is harmless and, in certain circum-
      stances, even beneficial. Reviews historical and recent
      legal cases and concludes that repeal of all obscenity
      legislation is highly desirable. Suggests that pornography
      should be criticized on aesthetic instead of ethical terms.
      (REVIEWS: *Books and Bookmen*, April 1973, p. 66; *Times
      Literary Supplement*, November 3, 1972, p. 1346)

53.   Sobel, Lester A. *Pornography, Obscenity and the Law*.
      New York: Facts on File, 1979.

      A general review and update of the issues surrounding
      the pornography controversy. Includes a discussion of
      the historical background, the role of organized crime
      and the effect of recent court decisions. An index and
      list of cases cited or abridged are included.

54.   Sunderland, Lane V. *Obscenity: The Court, the Congress
      and the President's Commission*. Washington, D.C.:
      American Enterprise Institute for Public Policy Research,
      1975. 127pp.

Analyzes the present state of obscenity law by examining four areas: (1) the 1973 Supreme Court decisions; (2) the status of the First Amendment protections as they relate to erotica; (3) the recommendations and inadequacies of the President's Commission on Obscenity and Pornography; and (4) the new laws proposed in Congress for the regulation of obscene materials. Argues that a balance between public morality and First Amendment protections must exist in good laws, but that some regulation seems desirable. Includes appendix of the major proposals of the 93rd Congress and selected bibliography. (REVIEW: *Choice*, October 1975, p. 986)

55. Sussman, Irving, and Cornelia Sussman. *How to Read a Dirty Book or the Way of the Pilgrim Reader*. Chicago: Franciscan Herald Press, 1966. 139pp.

Discusses reasons for and against reading pornographic literature. Distinguishes between a "dirty book" and non-literary pornography. The former is acceptable and can be read. The answer to the problem of pornography is to educate readers so that they can discriminate between the two. Christian arguments are presented against censorship. Appendix includes a list of recommended literary works, some of which have been considered obscene. (REVIEWS: *America*, April 23, 1966, p. 598; *Critic*, April/ May 1966, p. 76)

55a. Turan, Kenneth. *Sinema: American Pornographic Films and the People Who Make Them*. New York: Praeger Publishers Inc., 1974. 244pp.

Chronicles the history of the pornographic film industry in the United States. Contends that the erotic scenes in such major motion pictures as *Last Tango in Paris* could not have been presented without the previous production and distribution of thousands of sexploitation films. Interviews with key persons, including Russ Meyer, Marilyn Chambers and Harry Reems, are presented. 50 photos. Includes index. (REVIEW: *Publishers Weekly*, September 16, 1974, p. 56)

56. Wallace, Douglas H. "Pornography: Evaluational Reactions and Some Attitudinal Correlates." Ph.D. dissertation, Wayne State University, 1971. 145pp.

1083 subjects were individually exposed to 60 slides with sexual themes. Subjects rated slides on seven di-

mensions: offensiveness, sexual arousal, entertainment,
acceptance, availability, artistic value and educational
value. Responses were categorized into liberal-conserva-
tive groups with analysis indicating four particularly
important variables. They are: (1) general liberal-con-
servativism; (2) age; (3) religiosity; and (4) education.
Religiosity proved to be the best variable for predicting
responses. (*DAI* XXXII [1971])

57. Widmer, Eleanor, ed. *Freedom and Culture: Literary Cen-
     sorship in the 70s.* Belmont, California: Wadsworth,
     1970. 216pp.

     Contains more than 35 articles both historical and con-
     temporary on the subject of censorship, particularly as
     it relates to literary pornography. Devotes an entire
     section to the underlying principles of censorship, draw-
     ing from the works of Plato, Saint Paul, John Milton,
     Thomas Hobbes, John Stuart Mill, Thomas Jefferson and
     others. Contemporary figures are also included through
     the writings of Justice Brennan, Justice Douglas, Herbert
     Marcuse and Arthur Schlesinger, Jr. Broad cultural issues
     are discussed by such notables as Paul Goodman and Peter
     Michelson. Specific obscenity cases are reviewed includ-
     ing *Fanny Hill*, *Tropic of Cancer* and *Lady Chatterley's
     Lover*. Includes bibliography with list of books by U.S.
     and English authors that have been censored.

58. Williams, Tom M. *See No Evil: Christian Attitudes Toward
     Sex in Art and Entertainment.* Grand Rapids: Zondervan
     Publishing House, 1976. 103pp.

     Applies biblical principles to pornography and obscenity.
     The approach is to provide the "perplexed Christian" with
     some basic principles to apply to his own moral position
     against pornography. Pornography is defined and its
     harmful effects on society, especially on young people,
     are detailed. Alternatives to censorship, such as im-
     proving the movie rating code or prohibiting public
     display of pornographic publications, are presented.
     Finally, it is the Christian's responsibility to develop
     his own moral definition of pornography.

59. Zellinger, David A.; Howard L. Fromkin; Donald E. Speller;
     and Carol A. Kohn. *A Commodity Theory Analysis of the
     Effects of Age Restrictions upon Pornographic Materials.*
     West Lafayette, Indiana: Institute for Research in the
     Behavioral, Economic, and Management Sciences, 1974.
     16pp.

Applies the commodity theory to pornography. Concludes
that age restrictions placed on pornography do increase
its desirability, but materials labeled pornographic were
not more valued than the same materials not so identified.
64 college males participated. Results support the commodity theory prediction.

60.   Zurcher, Louis A., and R. George Kirkpatrick. *Citizens
      for Decency: Antipornography Crusades as Status Defense.*
      Austin: University of Texas Press, 1976.

Studies antipornography crusades as symbolic-status and
norm-oriented movements. Based upon in-depth case histories of two antipornography movements and interviews with
participants. Two communities, identified as Midville
and Southtown, were intensively studied. Detailed characteristics of those involved in antipornography campaigns,
labeled Conporns, and those not, the Proporns, are presented. Numerous findings are given, but the general
conclusion is that antipornography crusades are norm-
oriented movements and are symbols of broader social concerns for those involved. Appendix includes questionnaire. Index. Bibliography. (REVIEWS: *Choice*, November
1976, p. 1123; *Library Journal*, April 1, 1976, p. 917)

II

PSYCHOLOGICAL ARTICLES

61. Amoroso, Donald M., and Marvin Brown. "Problems in
    Studying the Effects of Erotic Material." *Journal of
    Sex Research* 9 (August 1973): 187-195.

    Examines the major problems confronting researchers
    who attempt to study the effects of pornographic mate-
    rials. The lack of standardized definitions and measure-
    ment techniques for certain basic concepts (i.e. sexual
    arousal or sexual stimuli) is discussed. The special
    sensitivity of the area and numerous problems involving
    appropriate control groups are enumerated. Concludes
    that more natural and realistic settings must be used in
    the study of sexual behavior, as opposed to the clinical
    "sex experiment."

62. Amoroso, Donald M.; Marvin Brown; Manfred Pruesse;
    Edward E. Ware; and Dennis W. Pilkey. "The Effects of
    Physiological Measurement and Presence of Others on
    Rating of Erotic Stimuli." *Canadian Journal of
    Behavioural Science* 4 (July 1972): 191-203.

    60 male undergraduates were exposed individually and
    in groups to slides of erotica and asked to rate them in
    three areas: (1) how pornographic the material was; (2)
    how stimulating it was; and (3) how pleasant or unpleas-
    ant it was. Results indicated that highly pornographic
    ratings correlated positively with highly stimulated
    ratings but negatively with pleasantness. Suggests that
    the "meaning" of pornography involves highly erotic and
    stimulating but relatively unpleasant material.

63. Athanasiou, Robert, and Phillip Shaver. "Correlates of
    Heterosexuals' Reactions to Pornography." *Journal of
    Sex Research* 7 (November 1971): 298-311.

    Utilizes certain items from a questionnaire distributed
    in the July 1969 *Psychology Today* to analyze reactions to

pornography as affected by attitudes, behavior and demographic characteristics. Concludes that both males and
females are aroused by some type of pornography and that
certain personal and social factors can be used to pre-
dict the degree of arousal.

63a. Baron, Robert A. "The Aggression-Inhibiting Influence of
Heightened Sexual Arousal." *Journal of Personality and
Social Psychology* 30 (September 1974): 318-322.

Male students were first angered and were then exposed
to erotic or neutral stimuli. Contrary to the predictions
of the experimenter, subjects subsequently permitted to
aggress against a confederate demonstrated reduced aggression following exposure to the erotic stimuli.

63b. Baron, Robert A. "Heightened Sexual Arousal and Physical
Aggression: An Extension to Females." *Journal of Research in Personality* 13 (March 1979): 91-102.

Female students were first angered and then exposed to
various types of erotic stimuli. Subjects were subsequently permitted to aggress against a female confederate.
Results indicated that aggression was reduced when subjects were exposed to mild erotica and increased when more
explicit erotica was employed. However, increases in
female's aggression were noted among erotic stimuli not
stimulating aggression in men.

63c. Baron, Robert A., and Paul A. Bell. "Sexual Arousal and
Aggression by Males: Effects of Type of Erotic Stimuli
and Prior Provocation." *Journal of Personality and
Social Psychology* 35 (February 1977): 79-87.

Investigates the possibility that aggression and sexual
arousal are curvilinearly related. Subjects were angered
and then exposed to neutral or various types of erotic
stimuli. Participants were subsequently permitted to
aggress against a confederate. Results indicated a decrease in aggression for those exposed to most erotic
materials, though an increase was noted in those exposed
to erotic passages.

63d. Brown, Marvin. "Viewing Time of Pornography." *Journal
of Psychology* 102 (May 1979): 83-95.

Male and female students were exposed to a series of
sexual slides varying in pornographic content to study
avoidance reaction. Male reactions were curvilinear show-

ing decreased viewing time with slides of highly pornographic content. Women showed no decrease in viewing
time.

64. Brown, Marvin; Donald M. Amoroso; and Edward E. Ware.
    "Behavioral Effects of Viewing Pornography." *Journal
    of Social Psychology* 98 (April 1976): 235-245.

    56 male college students were exposed to explicit slides
    of sexual activity. Most experienced some degree of sexual
    arousal and pleasure, but some were shocked and repelled.
    Many reported increased sexual activity, primarily mas-
    turbation, the same day the slides were viewed. However,
    no such increase was reported for the following week.

65. Brown, Marvin; Donald M. Amoroso; Edward E. Ware; Manfred
    Pruesse; and Dennis W. Pilkey. "Factors Affecting View-
    ing Time of Pornography." *Journal of Social Psychology*
    90 (June 1973): 125-135.

    Indicates that subjects (40 males) exposed to a series
    of pornographic slides chose to watch given slide longer
    if viewing the slide alone and unobserved. Also, as
    slides became more pornographic, subjects increased their
    viewing time. No curvilinear relationship between viewing
    time and the level of pornography was found, possibly be-
    cause no hard-core slides were presented.

66. Byrne, Donn; Fran Cherry; John Lamberth; and Herman E.
    Mitchell. "Husband-Wife Similarity in Response to
    Erotic Stimuli." *Journal of Personality* 41 (September
    1973): 385-394.

    Demonstrates that married couples display a statisti-
    cally significant similarity in their individual responses
    to pornography. Spouses also exhibited similar attitudes
    toward their judgment of pornography and their opinions
    about censorship. Also, authoritarianism was found to be
    an important factor in determining responses. 42 married
    couples participated in the study.

67. Byrne, Donn; Jeffrey D. Fisher; John Lamberth; and Herman
    E. Mitchell. "Evaluations of Erotica: Facts or Feelings."
    Journal of Personality and Social Psychology 29 (Janu-
    ary 1974): 111-116.

    Uses a reinforcement-affect model of evaluative responses
    to study reactions to pornography. Males exhibited both
    positive and negative affective responses, but women only
    negative affective responses, when making pornography

judgments. Other predictors include authoritarianism,
religious preference and church attendance. 64 married
subjects participated.

68. Colson, Charles E. "The Evaluation of Pornography; Effects
of Attitude and Perceived Physiological Reactions."
Archives of Sexual Behavior 3 (July 1974): 307-323.

23 male medical students and 28 male students at the
University of Illinois were exposed individually to four
literary passages. Two described heterosexual intercourse
and two pedophilia. False GSR feedback was employed, and
heart rate was monitored. Results indicated that when
informed that they are aroused by something they disapprove
of, individuals are more likely to label the stimuli obscene.

69. Cook, Royer F.; Robert H. Fosen; and Asher Pacht. "Pornography and the Sex Offender: Patterns of Previous Exposure and Arousal Effects of Pornographic Stimuli."
Journal of Applied Psychology 55 (December 1971): 503-
511.

66 criminal code violators and 63 sex offenders were
studied regarding past exposure to pornography and arousal
effects of erotic stimuli. Authors found sex offenders
had less exposure to pornography in childhood than criminal code violators, indicating a negative relationship
between exposure and tendency to commit a sex crime.
Also, talking of arousal in response to erotic stimuli
in general is less fruitful than talking about more specific responses to various types of sexual stimuli.

70. Crepault, Claude. "Sexual Fantasies and Visualization of
Pornographic Scenes." *Journal of Sex Research* 8 (May
1972): 154-155.

Presents two untested hypotheses concerning the role of
pornographic pictures on sexual fantasies. First, the
viewing of pornographic scenes may be the source of new
material for the subjects' sexual fantasies and actual
sex practices. Second, the vicarious satisfaction received from viewing pornographic scenes may serve as an
emotional catharsis which mediates between the world of
reality and that of fantasy. Confirmation of these hypotheses is being sought.

71. Davis, Keith E., and G. Nicholas Braucht. "Exposure to
Pornography, Character, and Sexual Deviance: A Retro-

spective Survey." *Journal of Social Issues* 29 (1973): 183-196.

A retrospective survey of 365 subjects was conducted to explore the relationship exposure to pornography bears to moral character and deviant sexual behavior. Positive relationships were found between sexual deviance and pornographic exposure, but no causal link was asserted. A positive relationship was also noted between poor character scores and exposure, but this relationship involved almost entirely those subjects exposed after the age of 17.

71a. Donnerstein, Edward; Marcia Donnerstein; and Ronald Evans. "Erotic Stimuli and Aggression: Facilitation or Inhibition." *Journal of Personality and Social Psychology* 32 (August 1975): 237-244.

Subjects were angered prior to or subsequent to exposure to mildly or highly erotic materials. Aggression decreased following exposure to mildly erotic materials and remained level following exposure to highly erotic materials. Subjects exposed to highly erotic materials and subsequently angered showed increased aggressive behavior.

71b. Donnerstein, Edward, and Gary Barrett. "Eroticism and Aggression." *Journal of Personality and Social Psychology* 36 (February 1978): 180-188.

Subjects were first angered then shown erotic or neutral films. Subsequently, subjects were permitted to aggress against a confederate. Findings indicate effects of erotica on males and females is similar, and exposure to such materials "does not, in and of itself, facilitate antisocial responses against females."

71c. Donnerstein, Edward, and John Hallam. "Facilitating Effects of Erotica on Aggression Against Women." *Journal of Personality and Social Psychology* 36 (November 1978): 1270-1277.

Subjects were first angered, then shown aggressive or erotic films. Subjects were subsequently permitted to aggress against a male or female target on two occasions separated by a short interval. Findings indicated that erotica facilitated aggression, particularly against women, on the second chance to aggress.

71d. Dunwoody, Vera, and Kathy Pezdek. "Factors Affecting the Sexual Arousal Value of Pictures." *Journal of Sex Research* 15 (November 1979): 276-284.

Examines factors in erotic photographs which affect
arousal value. These factors include position, view,
clothing and sex of model. Both male and female subjects
were exposed to erotic slides and results indicate that
all these factors significantly affect arousal value.

72. Englan, Ronald C., and C. Eugene Walker. "Male and Female
     Reactions to Erotic Literature." *Psychological Reports*
     32 (April 1973): 481-482.

     Refutes some earlier studies that found females re-
     sponded more strongly than males to hard-core pornography.
     80 subjects (40 men and 40 women) read and rated stories
     from two categories, erotic realism and hard-core pornog-
     raphy. No significant difference between responses by
     males and females was discovered. Results agree with re-
     search done by Kinsey.

72a. Fisher, William A., and Donn Byrne. "Sex Differences in
     Response to Erotica: Love Versus Lust." *Journal of
     Personality and Social Psychology* 36 (February 1978):
     117-125.

     Evaluates arousal, affective and evaluative responses
     by married and unmarried males and females to erotic
     films. Finds that females are aroused by erotica but no
     more than men are. Both men and women were more sexually
     aroused by suggested casual-sex themes than by a love or
     lust theme. Concludes that men and women do not respond
     differently in any of the measured response dimensions.

73. Gaughan, Edward J., and W. Michael. "College Student
     Rating of Arousal Value of Pornographic Photographs."
     *Proceedings of the 81st Annual Convention of the Ameri-
     can Psychological Association, Montreal, Canada* 8
     (1973): 409-410.

     Replicates an earlier study to determine the effects
     of direct administration of pornographic materials on
     subject's responses. 17 male and 29 female college stu-
     dents viewed and then rated the arousal effect of 19
     photographs of explicit sexual activities. Responses in-
     dicate that this type of pornography is not very stimu-
     lating.

74. Gibbans, F.X. "Sexual Standards and Reactions to Pornog-
     raphy: Enhancing Behavioral Consistency Through Self-
     Focused Attention." *Journal of Personality and Social
     Psychology* 36 (September 1978): 976-987.

Describes three studies which investigate the relationship between personal standards and self-awareness.
Different types of erotica and different tasks were used
in each study. Reactions to pornography viewed while
self-focused (in front of a mirror) or not self-focused
were recorded. Concludes that forced self-awareness
inhibits the response to the material.

75. Goldstein, Michael J. "Exposure to Erotic Stimuli and
    Sexual Deviance." *Journal of Social Issues* 29 (1973):
    197-219.

    Explores the relationship between exposure to pornog-
    raphy and development of normal or abnormal sexual activ-
    ity among rapists, pedophiles, homosexuals, transsexuals,
    heavy pornography users and a community control group.
    Results indicated that institutionalized sex offenders
    had been exposed to less pornography than had the control
    group. Degree of exposure to erotica is seen as a super-
    ficial part of general sexual development.

76. Gordon, Michael, and Robert R. Bell. "Medium and Hard-
    Core Pornography: A Comparative Analysis." *Journal of
    Sex Research* 5 (November 1969): 260-268.

    Compares "medium-core" and hard-core pornography. The
    former category can be legally defined as literature, but
    is primarily concerned with graphically described examples
    of sexual behavior. However, such sexual activity is
    typically limited to normal sexual intercourse, whereas
    hard-core pornography contains all varieties of sexual
    behavior. Other differences in theme and emphasis are
    detailed.

77. Halpern, James. "Projection: A Test of the Psychoanalytic
    Hypothesis." *Journal of Abnormal Psychology* 86 (Octo-
    ber 1977): 536-542.

    Investigates Freud's classical projection theory. 83
    male and 105 female college students completed the Sexual
    Defensiveness Scale and then selected a "most unfavorable
    other" from a group of photographs. After viewing porno-
    graphic items, each subject described himself and the
    unfavorable other. Highly sexually defensive subjects
    denied being aroused and projected such arousal on the
    unfavorable other. This supports the concept of classi-
    cal Freudian projection.

78. Hamrick, William S. "Fascination, Fear and Pornography:
    A Phenomenological Typology." *Man and World* 7 (Febru-
    ary 1974): 52-66.

Criticizes traditional definitions of pornography and
labels them "emotional obfuscation." Claims that oppo-
nents of pornography do not understand it enough to raise
viable objections to it. The structure of perceptual experience described by Merleau-Ponty is used to distinguish
between the pornographic and the erotic. Concludes that
pornography should be legalized because it does not cause
antisocial actions.

79. Houston, Judith. "Identifying Pornographic Materials with
    Judgment Analysis." *Journal of Experimental Education*
    42 (Summer 1974): 18-26.

    Reports a use of the Judgment Analysis (JAN) as a means
    for determining what is pornographic. Three groups of
    subjects (doctoral students, police officers and judges)
    were used. JAN was judged a successful method for iden-
    tification of policies. The technique was most effective
    in identifying the different policies of the three groups.

80. Houston, Judith; Samuel Houston; and E. LaMonte Ohlson.
    "On Determining Pornographic Material." *Journal of
    Psychology* 88 (November 1974): 277-287.

    74 subjects, including lawyers, police officers and
    doctoral students in psychology, were given 100 "stimulus
    profiles" depicting pornography and were asked to react
    by using an 11-item profile and rating the stimuli. The
    Judgment Analysis Technique (JAN) was used to evaluate the
    data. Significant clustering occurred around judgmental
    systems. Torture and flagellation were most often viewed
    as pornographic by all groups.

81. Howard, James L.; Myron B. Liptzin; and Clifford B. Reifler.
    "Is Pornography a Problem?" *Journal of Social Issues*
    29 (1973): 133-145.

    23 subjects were exposed to pornographic materials and
    films, 90 minutes a day for two weeks. Conclusions in-
    cluded: (1) continued exposure to pornography leads to
    decreased interest; (2) massive doses of pornography de-
    crease the arousal value of later pornography; and (3)
    detrimental changes in behavior and attitudes of subjects
    were not observed. Authors conclude pornography is an
    innocuous stimulus.

82. Izard, Carroll E., and Sanford Caplan. "Sex Differences
    in Emotional Responses to Erotic Literature." *Journal
    of Consulting and Clinical Psychology* 42 (June 1974):
    468.

224 undergraduates, 112 men and 112 women, were exposed to erotic and academic passages in two books.
Differential Emotions Scale was employed using interest,
joy, surprise, disgust, fear, guilt and sexual arousal
as subscales. Data confirmed expectation that males
would show greater interest, joy and sexual arousal
and women more disgust, but did not confirm hypothesis
that women would show greater fear and guilt.

82a. Jaffe, Yoram; Neil Malamuth; Joan Feingold; and Seymour
Feshbach. "Sexual Arousal and Behavioral Aggression."
Journal of Personality and Social Psychology 30 (Decem-
ber 1974): 759-764.

Male and female subjects were exposed to erotic or
neutral stimuli and then permitted to aggress against a
confederate by delivering electric shocks. Results revealed that aggression increased for both males and females exposed to erotica. It was noted that members of
the opposite sex received greater shocks.

83. Jakobovits, L.A. "Evaluational Reactions to Erotic Literature." *Psychological Reports* 16 (June 1965): 985-997.

Identifies two types of erotic literature, erotic
realism (ER) and hard-core obscenity (O). Ten stories
written specifically to match the characteristics of
each type were given to male and female subjects in two
studies. Study I revealed a high correlation between
subjects judging the classification of the stories as
either ER or O. Study II indicated that males and females
react differently to the two types of stories. Men are
more aroused by ER and women by O. A cumulative effect
from successive reading was also noted.

84. Kant, Harold S. "Exposure to Pornography and Sexual Behavior in Deviant and Normal Groups." *Corrective Psy-
chiatry and Journal of Social Therapy* 17 (1971): 5-17.

Correlates the degree of exposure to pornographic materials among specified groups to criminal and normal behavior. Samples included institutionalized sex offenders,
transsexuals, homosexuals, extensive pornography users
and male controls, all of whom were subjected to a
clinical interview. Findings included: (1) sex offenders
experienced less exposure to pornography as adolescents
than controls; (2) noninstitutionalized homosexuals had
greater exposure than controls; and (3) transsexuals,
"users of pornography" and homosexuals experience a cross-

over effect of less exposure during adolescence and
greater exposure in adulthood.

85. Kennedy, Eugene C. "Kind Words for the Porno-Researchers."
     Commonweal 93 (December 18, 1970): 292-293.

     Admonishes critics of the *Report of the Commission on
     Obscenity and Pornography* to study the report carefully
     before they denounce it. Contends that further research
     is needed in this area, but the present report represents
     accurate and professional study. The ethics and values
     of the investigators should not be maligned until the
     entire report is evaluated rationally.

86. Kercher, Glen A., and C. Eugene Walker. "Reactions of
     Convicted Rapists to Sexually Explicit Stimuli."
     Journal of Abnormal Psychology 81 (February 1973): 46-
     50.

     28 convicted rapists and 28 convicts who committed non-
     sexual crimes were exposed to nine slides of erotic mate-
     rial. Penile volume, galvanic skin responses (GSR) and
     semantic-differential rating scales were used to gather
     data. No differences in penile volume between sex offenders
     and others were noted, but rapists registered higher re-
     sponsiveness on GSR, and rated the erotic stimuli as
     significantly more negative. Contend that material was
     unpleasant and/or threatening to the rapists.

87. Kutschinsky, Berl. "Deviance and Criminality: The Case
     of Voyeur in a Peeper's Paradise." *Diseases of the
     Nervous System* 37 (March 1976): 145-151.

     Discusses the unexpected decline of criminal voyeurism,
     "peeping," in Denmark after legal prohibitions against
     pornography were eliminated. A detailed case study of one
     peeper, a 68-year-old sailor, is presented. Concludes
     that a deviant crime is primarily determined by external
     factors, i.e. the availability of opportunities and the
     law. A distinction is made between deviance and crimi-
     nality.

88. Lenes, Mark S., and Edward J. Hart. "The Influence of
     Pornography and Violence on Attitudes and Guilt."
     Journal of School Health 45 (October 1975): 447-451.

     Suggests that exposure to sexually explicit material
     does have some immediate emotional effect on most viewers.
     Violence in such materials produces the strongest reaction.
     Concludes, however, that there is no empirical basis for

linking pornography and declining cultural morality. No
conclusions were reached about long-range effect of continued exposure.

89. Levitt, Eugene E. "Pornography: Some New Perspectives on
    an Old Problem." *Journal of Sex Research* 5 (November
    1969): 247-259.

    Reviews studies and articles previously published on
    pornography. Classifies erotica into three categories:
    obscenity, "smut" and pornography. Pornography is distin-
    guished by the use of hard-core words and portrayals of
    actual sex acts such as intercourse. Concludes that it
    is impossible to determine if any form of visual erotica
    is "guilty or innocent of any charge."

90. Love, Robert E.; Lloyd R. Sloan; and Michael J. Schmidt.
    "Viewing Pornography and Sex Guilt: The Priggish, the
    Prudent, and the Profligate." *Journal of Consulting
    and Clinical Psychology* 44 (August 1976): 624-629.

    35 male undergraduates were divided into three groups
    using Mosher's Forced-Choice Guilt Inventory. Subjects
    viewed slides of erotica and were asked to rate them.
    Experimenters timed the slide changes for each subject.
    Low-sex-guilt subjects increased viewing time with in-
    creased obscenity ratings, while high-guilt subjects ex-
    perienced no time increases. Low-sex-guilt subjects rated
    slides as less obscene or disgusting. Data tend to sup-
    port Mosher's hypothesis.

90a. Malamuth, Neil M.; Seymour Feshbach; and Yoram Jaffe.
    "Sexual Arousal and Aggression: Recent Experiments and
    Theoretical Issues." *Journal of Social Issues* 33 (Spring
    1977): 110-133.

    Reviews the experimental literature with emphasis on
    sexual materials that may facilitate aggression. Proposes
    a model involving inhibitory and disinhibitory cures,
    which will help explain the many experiments which pro-
    duce inconsistent findings.

91. Merritt, C. Gary; Joel E. Gerstl; and Leonard A. LoSciuto.
    "Age and Perceived Effects of Erotica-Pornography: A
    National Sample Study." *Archives of Sexual Behavior* 4
    (November 1975): 605-621.

    Based on a national survey of 2486 adults on the effects
    of sexual materials, the authors develop a typology of
    the effects of erotica. Considerable heterogeneity is

noted throughout the sample on views regarding the effects
of erotica, but age factors seem to weigh heavily in
attitudinal changes. Speculation as to a "generation
gap" is advanced.

91a. Meyer, Timothy P. "The Effects of Sexually Arousing and
     Violent Films on Aggressive Behavior." *Journal of Sex
     Research* 8 (November 1972): 324-331.

     Male subjects were first angered and subsequently shown
     a violent or sexually arousing film. Subjects were then
     permitted to aggress against a confederate by delivering
     electric shocks. Results indicated increased aggression
     due to viewing violent or sexual films.

92. Moos, Rudolf H. "The Effects of Pornography: A Review of
    the Findings of the Obscenity and Pornography Commission."
    Comments on Contemporary Psychiatry 1 (1972): 123-131.

    Reviews the findings of the Commission on Obscenity and
    Pornography on behavioral, sexual, attitudinal, emotional
    and judgmental responses to erotic materials. Consensus
    is that most viewers are sexually aroused by erotic stim-
    uli. Exposure may result in temporary changes in emo-
    tional and attitudinal states, but sexual behavior is not
    affected. Reports that antisocial and criminal behavior
    is not shown to be related to experience with erotic
    materials. Explicit materials are less arousing, espe-
    cially for women.

93. Mosher, Donald L. "Sex Differences, Sex Experience, Sex
    Guilt, and Explicitly Sexual Films." *Journal of Social
    Issues* 29 (1973): 95-112.

    194 undergraduate males and 183 undergraduate females
    were shown two films, one involving coitus and one oral-
    genital sex. Differences in reaction were noted on the
    basis of sex difference, sex experience and sex guilt.
    Males reported an increase in general activation, and
    sexually experienced males were more aroused by the oral-
    genital presentation. Women had less positive and more
    negative effects, and were particularly activated by the
    film portraying coitus.

94. Osborn, Candice A., and Robert H. Pollack. "The Effects
    of Two Types of Erotic Literature on Physiological and
    Verbal Measures of Female Sexual Arousal." *Journal of
    Sex Research* 13 (November 1977): 250-256.

Discusses differences in sexual arousal of 12 female graduate students to two sets of erotic literature. One type was classified as hard-core pornography and the other as erotic realism. A vaginal photoplethysmograph was used to physiologically measure sexual arousal, and self-report scales were also completed by the subjects. Concludes that hard-core pornography produces greater arousal as measured by vaginal pressure pulse and subjective reports.

94a. Palmer, C. Eddie. "Pornographic Comics: A Content Analysis." *Journal of Sex Research* 15 (November 1979): 285-297.

100 porno-comics were examined using categories developed by the Kronhausens. Concluded that comics portray both men and women as being sexually aggressive and possessing substantial sexual appetites. Also noted was considerable sex-role stereotyping.

95. Pincus, Steven, and L.K. Waters. "Effect of Age Restrictions and Pornographic Content on Desirability of Reading Material." *Psychological Reports* 38 (June 1976): 943-947.

Evaluates the combinations of age restrictions and pornographic content on the desirability of reading the material as indicated by 96 male and 96 female subjects. Age restriction had a significant effect, regardless of whether the book was labeled pornographic. However, the desirability for a pornographic book did not differ significantly with or without age restrictions. Concludes that a social desirability response-set may have played a part in the latter results.

96. Reed, John P., and Robin S. Reed. "Consensus and Dissensus in Pornography Definitions: A Content Analysis." *International Behavioural Scientist* 5 (September 1973): 1-12.

Compares legal and individual definitions of pornography. Reviews federal court definitions from 1870 to 1970. Early court decisions stressed "effects," but recently "definitional qualifications and exceptions" have taken precedence. 132 college students' individual definitions of pornography were studied and compared to legal definitions. Students were generally more conservative than the courts and appeared to be 30 to 40 years behind current court definitions.

97. Reed, John P., and Robin S. Reed. "P.R.U.D.E.S. (Pornog-
     raphy Research Using Direct Erotic Stimuli)." *Journal
     of Sex Research* 8 (August 1972): 237-246.

     Examines the differing reactions to pornography of in-
     dividuals and of groups comprised of similar individuals.
     Individuals tended to produce a relative definition of
     pornography, but groups most often gave content and effect
     definitions. Minority views were eliminated in the group
     process. Suggests that pornography research must not be
     limited to individual responses, but must also consider
     the individual in his various social groups.

98. Reifler, Clifford B.; James Howard; Morris A. Lipton;
     Myron B. Liptzin; and Donald E. Widmann. "Pornography:
     An Experimental Study of Effects." *American Journal of
     Psychiatry* 128 (November 1971): 575-582.

     23 subjects were exposed to a "smorgasbord" of porno-
     graphic materials, 90 minutes a day for three weeks. A
     before-and-after study was conducted on subjects viewing
     hard-core stag films. A second study was conducted to
     see what happened on a day-to-day basis to subjects ex-
     posed to the materials for three weeks. Results indicated
     that subjects became satiated with pornography, and that
     intensive erotic stimulation had no lasting effect on
     behavior or attitude.

99. Rosen, Lawrence, and Stanley Turner. "Exposure to Pornog-
     raphy: An Exploratory Study." *Journal of Sex Research*
     5 (November 1969): 235-246.

     Considers the consumer of pornography. People exposed
     to pornography were equally likely to view legal or il-
     legal pornography. Two important variables in determining
     who sees or reads pornography are demographic (age, sex,
     religion, marital status) and behavioral (reading books).

100. Sanford, Donald A. "Patterns of Sexual Arousal in Hetero-
     sexual Males." *Journal of Sex Research* 10 (May 1974):
     150-155.

     Summarizes the results of exposure to erotic films and
     slides. Films produced more penile volume changes than
     slides presenting the same activity. The most arousing
     themes were those showing heterosexual intercourse. Con-
     cludes that the activity is more important than sex of the
     performers in determining sexual arousal.

101. Schaefer, Halmuth H., and Aloma H. Colgan. "The Effect
     of Pornography on Penile Tumescence as a Function of
     Reinforcement and Novelty." *Behavior Therapy* 8 (Novem-
     ber 1977): 938-946.

     Employing a device to measure penile erection, ten
     males were subjected to standard and novel pornography
     for six experimental sessions. After exposure, control
     groups were asked to read nonpornographic material while
     experimental subjects were to ejaculate. Responding
     increased over trials for group allowed to ejaculate,
     and novel pornography received higher ratings than stan-
     dard pornography in general. Cautions that experiments
     using the same pornographic stimuli repeatedly on the
     same subjects may have inconclusive findings due to
     habituation.

102. Schill, Thomas; Ron Evans; and Dennis Scott Drain.
     "Effects of Approval or Disapproval on Reading Behavior
     of High- and Low-Guilt Subjects." *Journal of Consult-
     ing and Clinical Psychology* 43 (February 1975): 104.

     Tests Donald Mosher's hypothesis that censure should
     "enhance viewing of an erotic magazine for low- but not
     high-guilt subjects." 24 high- and 24 low-guilt sub-
     jects were predisposed by the use of a confederate to
     view the available erotica in a negative, positive or
     neutral light. Disapproval produced the longer viewing
     times, but data did not confirm Mosher's hypothesis.

103. Schmidt, Gunter; Sigusch Volkmar; and Siegrid Schafer.
     "Responses to Reading Erotic Stories: Male-Female
     Differences." *Archives of Sexual Behavior* 2 (1973):
     181-199.

     Evaluates responses of men and women to erotic stories.
     120 female and 120 male college students participated.
     Only minimal differences in reactions between sexes
     were observed. Emotional reactions included a general
     activation, certain avoidance reactions and an increase
     in emotional instability. Women experienced more in-
     creased sexual activity and drive during the 24 hours
     after the experiment than men.

104. Stauffer, John, and Richard Frost. "Male and Female
     Interest in Sexually-Oriented Magazines." *Journal of
     Communication* 26 (Winter 1976): 25-30.

     Compares responses of males to *Playboy* to those of
     women to *Playgirl*. Men rated the nude photo essay the

most interesting, but women placed the male nude photo
essay contained in *Playgirl* much lower. This disparity
may result from social pressures and traditions and does
not indicate a lesser response by women to erotic materials.

105.   Stoller, Robert J. "Pornography and Perversion."
       Archives of General Psychiatry 22 (June 1970): 490-
       499.

       An exploration into how pornography can aid in the
       investigations of perversions. An example of trans-
       vestite pornography is chosen, and a case history is
       presented. Stress is placed on the fact that pornography
       for one person may not be pornography to another; hostile
       fantasies may be disguised but active in the pornography
       itself.

106.   Thompson, Joseph J., and Paul W. Dixon. "A Power Func-
       tion Between Ratings of Pornographic Stimuli and Psy-
       chophysical Responses in Young Normal Adult Women."
       Perceptual and Motor Skills 38 (June 1974): 1236-1238.

       Details results of an experiment which used a galvanic
       skin response instrument to measure psychophysical re-
       sponses to a set of pornographic pictures viewed by ten
       female subjects. A power function for the pornographic
       stimuli was obtained by computing algebraic averages and
       plotting them. Subjects demonstrated mathematically
       predictable responses to the ranked pornographic stimuli.

107.   Wallace, Douglas H., and Gerald Wehmer. "Pornography
       and Attitude Change." *Journal of Sex Research* 8 (May
       1971): 116-125.

       Concludes that a voluntary exposure for three hours
       to erotic and pornographic pictures does not result in
       a change in the subject's attitude toward censorship or
       pornographic materials in general. No significant change
       in subject's moral values was detected. Future studies
       should consider possible long-term effects and changes.

108.   Ware, Edward E.; Marvin Brown; Donald M. Amoroso; Dennis
       W. Pilkey; and Manfred Pruesse. "The Semantic Meaning
       of Pornographic Stimuli." *Canadian Journal of Behav-
       ioural Science* 4 (July 1972): 204-209.

       40 subjects between the ages of 18 and 25 viewed slides
       of erotica and were asked to rate them on the basis of

11 semantic differential scales. Included were the
dimensions of pleasantness, benefit, goodness, stimulation, activity, hotness, strength, heaviness and seriousness. The "looking time" for each slide was also recorded. Results indicated that "highly pornographic
slides were considered bad, unpleasant, dirty and harmful, and to a lesser degree as active, hot and stimulating."

109. Waring, E.M., and J.J. Jeffries. "Conscience of a
      Pornographer." *Journal of Sex Research* 10 (February
      1974): 40-46.

      Describes a clinical case history of a professional
      pornographer. Although treatments are detailed, the
      intent is to provide insights into the mind of the por-
      nographer. Unconscious guilt feelings are evident and
      the production of pornography is concluded to be a form
      of sexual deviation which reflects "unconscious motiva-
      tions and unresolved conflicts."

110. Wehmer, Gerald, and Douglas H. Wallace. "Pornography
      and Attitude Change." *Proceedings of the Annual Con-
      vention of the American Psychological Association* 5
      (1970): 405-406.

      Considers the relationship between exposure to obscene
      materials and attitude change. 40 male undergraduates
      viewed and rated packets of photographs dealing with
      sexual themes. Approximately one-third were considered
      legally obscene. Results indicate that a voluntary ex-
      posure to pornographic pictures does not result in a
      change in a person's attitude toward such materials. No
      significant disruption of the subject's moral values was
      observed.

110a. White, Leonard A. "Erotica and Aggression: The Influence
      of Sexual Arousal, Positive Affect, and Negative Affect
      on Aggressive Behavior." *Journal of Personality and
      Social Psychology* 37 (April 1979): 591-601.

      Male subjects were angered and then exposed to positive
      and negative erotic stimuli. Subjects were then allowed
      to aggress against a target by delivering electric shocks.
      Findings indicate a reduction of aggression after ex-
      posure to negative erotic stimuli.

111. Wilson, W. Cody, and Herbert I. Abelson. "Experience
      with and Attitudes Toward Explicit Sexual Materials."
      Journal of Social Issues 29 (1973): 19-39.

Interviews were conducted on experience with explicit
sexual material with a national probability sample of
adults age 21 and older. Findings include the following:
(1) explicit sexual materials are widespread in the population; (2) little sense can be made of the judicial
notion of "contemporary community standards"; and (3)
attitudes toward and experience with explicit sexual
materials vary widely.

112. Zellinger, David A.; Howard L. Fromkin; Donald E. Speller;
      and Carol A. Kohn. "A Commodity Theory Analysis of
      the Effects of Age Restrictions upon Pornographic
      Materials." *Journal of Applied Psychology* 60 (Febru-
      ary 1975): 94-99.

      Explores the commodity theory prediction that restrict-
      ing a commodity, i.e. pornographic materials, increases
      its desirability. 64 male undergraduate students were
      given an experimental booklet which allegedly contained
      four statements from book covers. Some statements con-
      tained age restrictions and some contained information
      on how pornographic the book was. Results indicated
      that age restrictions increased product desirability.

112a. Zillmann, D.; J.L. Hoyt; and K.D. Day. "Strength and
      Duration of the Effect of Aggressive, Violent, and
      Erotic Communication on Subsequent Aggressive Behav-
      ior." *Communication Research* 1 (July 1974): 286-306.

      Subjects were angered, exposed to violent or erotic
      films and then shown a neutral communication. Subse-
      quently, they were permitted to aggress against a con-
      federate. Results indicate increased aggression only
      for those viewing the erotic film.

112b. Zillmann, D., and B.S. Sapolosky. "What Mediates the
      Effect of Mild Erotica on Hostile Behavior in Males."
      Journal of Personality and Social Psychology 35
      (August 1977): 587-596.

      Individuals were provoked and then exposed to mild
      erotic stimuli. Annoyance and retaliatory behavior
      against a confederate was subsequently measured. Results
      indicate a decrease in annoyance following exposure to
      mild erotic materials but no change in strength in re-
      taliatory behavior.

III

SOCIOLOGICAL ARTICLES

113. Bachy, Victor. "Danish 'Permissiveness' Revisited."
     Journal of Communication 26 (Winter 1976): 40-43.

     Questions the conclusion that the legalization of
     pornography in Denmark in 1969 had beneficial effects
     on society, i.e. a decline in sex crimes. Argues that
     statistics for the period 1969-1974 are inconclusive
     and do not document any improvement. Argues that the
     availability of pornography has altered the concept of
     decency. Concludes that pornography should not be le-
     galized, because of its close relationship with violence,
     prostitution and drugs.

114. Barnett, Walter. "Corruption of Morals--The Underlying
     Issue of the Pornography Commission Report." *Law and
     the Social Order* 1971 (1971): 189-243.

     Reviews the findings of the Commission on Obscenity
     and Pornography. Questions whether it is proper for
     society to use legal means to regulate moral standards.
     The principles presented in John Stuart Mill's essay
     "On Liberty" are used to justify the conclusion that
     society must limit itself to controlling behavior that
     is demonstrably harmful to other citizens.

115. Berger, Alan S.; William Simon; and John H. Gagnon.
     "Youth and Pornography in Social Context." *Archives
     of Sexual Behavior* 2 (December 1973): 279-308.

     Data were derived from two sources: a survey of 473
     young people from a working-class community, and an
     analysis of items on pornography from a study of 1177
     college students. Authors conclude that pornography is
     not a powerful behavior-shaping force, but a component
     of an individual's media consumption. Sexual behavior
     is seen as being influenced more by social position and
     personal characteristics.

116. Berns, Walter. "On Pornography: I--Pornography vs.
      Democracy: The Case for Censorship." *Public Interest*
      22 (Winter 1971): 3-24.

      Draws a connection between shame, self-restraint and
      self-government or democracy. Argues there is a poli-
      tical and social danger in allowing pornography to
      flourish uncensored. Censorship is seen as maintaining
      the distinction between art and "trash." The distinction
      can and must be made to guarantee continued democracy
      in America.

117. Bickel, Alexander; Stanley Kauffmann; Wilson Carey
      McWilliams; and Marshall Cohen. "On Pornography:
      II--Dissenting and Concurring Opinions." *Public In-
      terest* 22 (Winter 1971): 25-44.

      Responses are given to an earlier article by Walter
      Berns (see 116). Bickel argues for more local and state
      involvement with censorship and less federal court ac-
      tion. Kauffmann considers censorship of pornography
      "anticivil and anticivilized." McWilliams contends the
      only safe and useful censorship is self-censorship.
      Cohen agrees only that public nuisances can be prohib-
      ited by law, but is against the type of censorship pro-
      posed by Berns.

118. Birkelbach, Ronald D., and Louis A. Zurcher, Jr. "Some
      Socio-Political Characteristics of Anti-Pornography
      Campaigners." *Sociological Symposium* 4 (Spring 1970):
      13-22.

      Presents some of the socio-political characteristics
      of active participants in *ad hoc* antipornography groups.
      Structured interviews were conducted in two cities iden-
      tified as Southtown and Midville. Antipornography re-
      spondents were labeled Conporn and anticensorship re-
      spondents were designated Proporn. Conporn participants
      were found to be middle-income, older, less well-edu-
      cated, less often in professional occupations, more ac-
      tive in organized religion, more politically conserva-
      tive, and more authoritarian.

119. Bonfield, Arthur E. "Nudity in the Theatre: A Case
      Study in Legal Analysis." *Educational Theatre Journal*
      28 (May 1976): 151-173.

      Reports action taken by the University of Iowa to pro-
      hibit a dance troupe from performing a nude work in a
      campus auditorium. The production was prevented but

subsequent "corrective action" was taken to ensure artistic freedom in the future. A detailed legal memo-
randum referring to Supreme Court decisions, lower
federal courts and especially Iowa statutes and cases
is included.

120.) Bonniwell, Bernard L.   "The Social Control of Pornog-
       raphy and Sexual Behavior." *Annals of the American
       Academy of Political and Social Science* 397 (September
       1971): 97-104.

       Argues that pornography must be seen as a form of
       education which influences emotions of considerable
       power and as such must be regulated in the society.
       Contends that mass media have made erotica a public
       phenomenon and a destructive force, and consequently,
       it is necessary to devise a monitoring system to control
       the dissemination of such material in the mass media.
       A five-point "National Educational Monitoring Center"
       proposal is advanced.

121.   Bosmajian, Haig A.   "Obscenity, Sexism, and Freedom of
       Speech." *College English* 39 (March 1978): 812-819.

       Argues that Supreme Court decisions on obscenity are
       sexist. By accepting the argument that there is a con-
       nection between pornography and antisocial, criminal
       behavior, the Court allows restrictions on such mate-
       rials. However, the criminal acts--rape, peeping and
       exhibitionism--are committed by men, not women. Con-
       sequently, the Supreme Court decisions are determining
       what adult females can read, even though no correlation
       has been established between pornography and criminal
       acts by women.

122.   Bouras, James. "In the Realm of the Censors." *Film
       Comment* 13 (January 1977): 32-33.

       Reports attempts by the U.S. Customs to recall a for-
       eign film, *In the Realm of the Senses*, previously al-
       lowed to enter the United States and to prevent its
       public showing. The U.S. Attorney's office, however,
       countermanded this recall demand and a Federal District
       Court enjoined Customs from taking any actions against
       the film. Excerpts from the court hearing are ap-
       pended.

123.   Brown, Coke; Joan Anderson; Linda Burggraf; and Neal
       Thompson. "Community Standards, Conservatism, and

Judgments of Pornography." *Journal of Sex Research*
14 (May 1978): 81-95.

Attempts to determine if a community standard of obscenity does exist. 25 pictures of various erotic contents were judged to be pornographic or not pornographic
by subjects chosen at random in a community. Results
suggested the possibility of establishing a representative community standard, but only in a small community.
Wilson and Patterson's Conservatism Scale was also used
and showed that conservatism is a major factor in predicting judgments of pornography.

124.   Burt, Mary E. Hamilton. "Use of Pornography by Women:
       A Critical Review of the Literature." *Case Western
       Reserve Journal of Sociology* 8 (September 1976): 1-16.

Reviews the research on sex-oriented materials from
1965 to 1972. Six categories are considered: (1) definition of and exposure to sex-oriented materials; (2)
analysis of the market for erotica; (3) demographic
characteristics of users; (4) personality correlates
and responses to erotica; (5) exposure and attitudes
toward erotica; and (6) emotional and physiological
responses of men and women. The final category has the
least amount of research. Further research is needed
to show how women's responses to erotica are affected by
social and cultural factors.

125.   Calderone, Mary S. "Pornography as a Public Health
       Problem." *American Journal of Public Health and the
       Nation's Health* 62 (March 1972): 374.

Pornography is examined briefly from the perspective
of public health. The key question examined is when and
how eroticism may be misused by a significant portion
of the population so that it becomes a danger to the
society itself. Emphasis is placed on the contributions
of the social sciences.

126.   Carlin, John C. "The Rise and Fall of Topless Radio."
       Journal of Communication 26 (Winter 1976): 31-37.

Questions the authority of the Federal Communications
Commission (FCC) to fine or refuse to renew the license
of radio or television stations because of allegedly
obscene programming. Legal precedents do establish such
authority. The action by the FCC against the Sonderling
Broadcasting Corporation for airing sexually explicit
talk shows, "topless radio," is detailed. As a result,
such programs have been stopped.

127. Court, J.H. "Pornography and Sex Crimes--Re-Evaluation in Light of Recent Trends Around the World." *International Journal of Criminology and Penology* 5 (May 1977): 129-157.

Discusses the causal connections between exposure to pornography and sex crimes. Argues that the *Report of the Commission on Obscenity and Pornography* was misleading and based on inadequate evidence. Asserts that myths have developed based on the *Report*, including: (1) free access to erotica leads to boredom with the material; (2) children can be protected from erotica while adults have free access; and (3) sex crimes decrease when erotica is available. Reanalyzes data from Denmark, and examines data from Sweden, the U.S., New Zealand, Australia, Singapore and England.

128. Dobbins, Howard W. "Regulation of Adult Theaters by Zoning." *Public Management* 59 (February 1977): 14-16.

Reports the decision of the Supreme Court in *Young* v. *American Mini Theaters, Inc.* City ordinances that restrict the location of establishments which exhibit adult movies or sell other sexually explicit materials are not unconstitutional. Zoning regulations can be used to control adult theaters. Excerpts from the majority decision are included.

129. Douglas, Melvyn; Florence Eldridge; Fredric March; and Henry Wheeler. "On Porno and Violence." *Center Report* 6 (December 1973): 28-30.

A general discussion of the possible effects censorship cases have on the arts, particularly film and theater. The relationship of public concern over violence to public concern over pornography is analyzed, and concern is expressed over the possibility of censorship spilling over into the political domain.

130. Feldman, Charles, and Stanley Tickton. "Obscene/Indecent Programming: Regulation of Ambiguity." *Journal of Broadcasting* 20 (Spring 1976): 273-282.

Reports two important Federal Communications Commission (FCC) decisions, *Sonderling Broadcasting Corp.* (41 FCC 2nd 777) and *Pacifica Foundation* (51 FCC 2nd 430). In both cases, portions of radio talk shows were found to be obscene, and punitive action was taken by the FCC against the stations. Concludes that such decisions by a federal regulatory agency should best be left to the federal courts.

131. Ferlemann, Mimi. "Pornography." *Menninger Perspective*
      2 (April 1971): 2-7.

          Reviews the findings of the Commission on Obscenity
      and Pornography. Extensive comments are provided by
      Dr. Edward Greenwood, a member of the Commission and a
      consultant to the Menninger Foundation. He suggests
      that education, not legislation, is the only effective
      method of controlling pornography. Warns that any
      legislation which results in limiting the First or Four-
      teenth Amendment is more dangerous to society than por-
      nography.

132. French, Michael R. "Sex in the Current Cinema." *Kansas
      Quarterly* 4 (Spring 1972): 39-46.

          Indicates the difficulty of distinguishing between
      pornographic and legitimate movies. One distinction is
      that pornographic films present sex as "mindlessly plea-
      surable," while legitimate movies often treat sex as
      "profoundly disturbing." Contends that contemporary
      movies continue to combine sex and violence and to ex-
      plain sexual behavior in Freudian terms.

133. Friedman, Jane M. "Erotica, Censorship, and the United
      States Post Office Department." *Michigan Academician*
      4 (Summer 1971): 7-16.

          Labels the U.S. Post Office Department an "anti-
      pollutant for our nation's mailstream." Cites opening
      of sealed mail and identifying of persons ordering por-
      nographic materials as examples of abuses by this fed-
      eral agency. Warns that these administrative procedures
      could be used to enforce censorship of any material con-
      sidered "objectionable."

134. Fromkin, Howard L., and Timothy C. Brock. "Erotic Ma-
      terials: A Commodity Theory Analysis of the Enhanced
      Desirability That May Accompany Their Unavailability."
      Journal of Applied Social Psychology 3 (July 1973):
      219-231.

          Applies contemporary commodity theory to the present
      trends toward restriction of pornographic materials.
      Discusses the assumptions of commodity theory in general,
      and then demonstrates how treating pornography as a
      commodity affects our approaches to regulation of such
      materials. Argues that restricting availability and
      attempting to silence distributors only serve to make
      the product more desirable, particularly to the young.

135. Funston, Richard. "Pornography and Politics: The
     Court, the Constitution, and the Commission."
     Western Political Quarterly 24 (December 1971): 635-
     652.

     Traces the U.S. Supreme Court's attempts to define
     "obscenity" and to determine why it should be regulated.
     Concludes there are "serious defects" in all legal tests
     for obscenity suggested by the Court and in each of the
     constitutional justifications presented for its regu-
     lation. The difficulty of applying the First Amendment
     to artistic expression is discussed.

136. Gagnon, John H., and William Simon. "Pornography--Rag-
     ing Menace or Paper Tiger?" *Trans-Action* 4 (July-
     August 1967): 41-47.

     Argues that pornography itself is not dangerous, but
     that the attempts to deal with it represent a definite
     threat to the freedom of thought and speech. Standards
     to judge pornography remain elusive and are too depen-
     dent on members of the Supreme Court. Contends that
     censorship of pornography can lead to repression of
     ideas.

137. Gans, Herbert J. "*Deep Throat*: The Pornographic Film
     Goes Public." *Social Policy* 4 (July-August 1973):
     119-121.

     Reviews the film *Deep Throat*. Contends that wider
     audiences, specifically liberated middle-class couples,
     are now viewing pornographic films. Such films and
     pornography are considered victimless crimes, and no
     need for censorship is apparent.

138. Garson, Helen S. "John Hawkes and Elements of Pornog-
     raphy." *Journal of Popular Culture* 10 (Summer 1976):
     150-155.

     Considers whether the novels of John Hawkes (*Second
     Skin* and *The Lime Twig*) are pornographic. Identifies
     eight of the major criteria for pornography, as defined
     in *Pornography and the Law*, in his novels. Concludes
     that these elements are used to show life as perceived
     by the author.

139. Gill, Brendan. "Justice is Blind--and Dirty-minded."
     Film Comment 12 (July 1976): 6.

     Cites current attempts by "fumbling and bungling" leg-
     islators, judges and public prosecutors to further re-

strict the protection of the First Amendment. The conviction of Harry Reems for his involvement in *Deep
Throat* and the prosection of Al Goldstein for violating
the community standards of Wichita, Kansas, are cited as
examples. The Supreme Court's acceptance of zoning
ordinances designed to restrict the availability of
adult materials is also attacked.

140. Glassman, Marc B. "Community Standards of Patent Offensiveness: Public Opinion Data and Obscenity Law."
Public Opinion Quarterly 42 (Summer 1978): 161-170.

Reviews available opinion polls that have been conducted to establish a community standard with regard to
obscenity. None is particularly useful or accurate.
This study analyzes a survey conducted in 1970 by the
Commission on Obscenity and Pornography. Concludes that
some explicitly sexual material is acceptable in all
types of communities. Larger metropolitan areas are
more liberal, but most other communities regard as obscene any depictions which go beyond nudity and intercourse.

141. Hamalian, Leo. "The Secret Careers of Samuel Roth."
Journal of Popular Culture 1 (Spring 1968): 317-338.

Biographical account of the career of Samuel Roth.
His legal fame results from the Supreme Court decision
in *Roth* v. *United States*, which delineated the "prurient
interest" test for obscenity. Roth's unauthorized re-
production and sale of D.H. Lawrence's *Lady Chatterley's
Lover* is only one example of such activity. He is labeled an "Unblushing Pirate." The difficulty in determining what Roth wrote and what he plagiarized is emphasized.

142. Hausknecht, Murray. "The Problem of Pornography."
Dissent 25 (Spring-Summer 1978): 193-208.

Reviews the findings of the Commission on Obscenity
and Pornography. Although the Commission overlooks the
long-range effects of pornography, there is still no
empirical evidence of such effects. Justification of
censorship based on the alleged harm it causes is un-
acceptable to liberals. However, the use of zoning
laws to deal with pornography is a workable alternative.

143. Holbrook, David. "Politics of Pornography." *Political
Quarterly* 48 (1977): 44-53.

Argues against the availability of pornography and
urges serious public debate on the problem. Pornography is viewed as "immoral and harmful." Public
opinion is seen as being manipulated by producers and as
a result, serious social and political consequences and
an "inverted moral atmosphere" are developing.

144. Houston, Judith; Samuel Houston; and E. LaMonte Ohlson.
      "The Atypicality of Pornography and Public Policy: A
      Pilot Investigation." *Psychology; A Journal of Human
      Behavior* 11 (November 1974): 3-7.

      Reports an experiment which exposed 28 doctoral stu-
      dents to 100 pictorial representations, primarily of
      sexual activity. The Judgment Analysis Technique was
      used to analyze the responses. It was judged to be a
      successful means of determining what constitutes pornog-
      raphy.

145. Karp, David A. "Hiding in Pornographic Bookstores--Re-
      consideration of Nature of Urban Anonymity." *Urban
      Life and Culture* 1 (January 1973): 427-451.

      Details behavior of persons frequenting adult book-
      stores. Persons attempted to hide or obscure their
      destination on approaching such stores, and their inten-
      tions once inside. No contact, verbal or physical, was
      normally observed between patrons or between a patron
      and the cashier. The social situation within porno-
      graphic bookstores is very standardized, and privacy is
      highly valued and protected.

146. Katz, Bill. "The Pornography Collection." *Library
      Journal* 96 (December 1971): 4060-4066.

      Entertains the idea of building a pornography collec-
      tion as a way to explore the various selection problems
      confronting the librarian. Reviews basic Supreme Court
      decisions broadening and liberalizing obscenity law and
      cases involving librarians and dissatisfied library
      boards.

147. Kenyon, F.E. "Pornography, Law and Mental Health."
      British Journal of Psychiatry 126 (March 1975): 225-
      233.

      A general review of the pornography issue as it centers
      in Great Britain. Particular attention is paid to: (1)
      findings of recent surveys and reports; (2) cultural as-
      pects as they pertain to traditions, politics and socio-

logical value; (3) legal aspects; (4) pathological aspects; and (5) general effects of pornography. Contends
that evidence does not suggest harm to one's mental
health, and advocates better education, especially for
children.

148. Kirkpatrick, R. George. "Collective Consciousness and
      Mass Hysteria: Collective Behavior and Anti-Pornog-
      raphy Crusades in Durkheimian Perspective." *Human
      Relations* 28 (February 1975): 63-84.

      Employing a Durkheimian approach to collective behav-
      ior, the natural history of two antipornography organi-
      zations is studied with particular attention focused on
      the nature of the reaction to the sale of pornography.
      Concludes that the law itself does not determine the
      type of reaction from a group when it is violated;
      rather, the severity of group reaction depends on how
      serious the group perceives the threat to the collective
      consciousness to be.

149. Kirkpatrick, R. George. "Moral Indignation and Repressed
      Sexuality: The Sociosexual Dialectics of Antipornog-
      raphy Crusades." *The Psychoanalytic Review* 61 (Spring
      1974): 141-149.

      Studies participants in two antipornography campaigns.
      Most crusaders were predominantly lower middle class.
      Antipornography campaigners were also found to be highly
      repressed sexually, extremely intolerant of deviant be-
      havior and willing to inflict punishment. Concludes that
      antipornography campaigns result from repressed sexual-
      ity among participants.

150. Klotman, Phyllis R. "Racial Stereotypes in Hard Core
      Pornography." *Journal of Popular Culture* 5 (Summer
      1971): 221-235.

      Describes racial stereotypes found in American porno-
      graphic comic books. Various stereotypes are identified
      (i.e. Buffoon, Comic Stud, Black Beast, etc.), and it is
      concluded that race is not normally significant in the
      type of sexual activity or behavior portrayed. Blacks
      often, however, appear as nonparticipants in the actual
      sexual activity. The comics considered were published
      between 1900 and 1950.

151. Kutschinsky, Berl. "The Effect of Easy Availability
      of Pornography on the Incidence of Sex Crimes: The

Danish Experience." *Journal of Social Issues* 29
(1973): 163-181.

An examination of the causal links between readily
available pornography and increases or decreases in sex
crimes in Copenhagen. Unexpected outcome was that high
availability of pornography was the probable direct
cause of decreases in child molestation.

152. Kutschinsky, Berl. "Eroticism Without Censorship:
      Sociological Investigations on the Production and
      Consumption of Pornographic Literature in Denmark."
      International Journal of Criminology and Penology 1
      (August 1973): 217-225.

A review of the consumption of pornography in Copenhagen before and after the liberalization of pornography
laws. Examining book consumption, argues that the major
upsurge in production and consumption occurred in the
1960s, and following total legal access in 1967, consumption increased temporarily, then decreased. Believes
the satiation effect has now taken hold.

153. Lewittes, Don J., and William L. Simmons. "Impression
      Management of Sexually Motivated Behavior." *Journal
      of Social Psychology* 96 (June 1975): 39-44.

Indicates that subjects (130 college males) observed
buying "girlie" magazines (*Playboy*, *Penthouse* and *Oui*)
exhibited certain behaviors designed to lessen potential
negative reactions from others. Typically, a bag was re-
quested or other items were also purchased. Such actions
are examples of face-saving strategies.

154. McCormack, Thelma. "Machismo in Media Research: A
      Critical Review of Research on Violence and Pornog-
      raphy." *Social Problems* 25 (June 1978): 544-555.

Attempts to account for the discrepancies between the
findings of three major investigations: the National
Commission on the Causes and Prevention of Violence
(1969), the Commission on Obscenity and Pornography
(1970), and the Surgeon General's Report on Television
and Social Behavior (1972). The major conflicting findings
are that the effects of pornography are harmless, but that
the effects of violence are significant and justify censorship. Concludes that all three investigations were
sexually biased and suggests the use of reference-group
theory.

155. McKay, Robert B. "One Nation Divisible--With Pornography for Some." *Bulletin of the Copyright Society* 21 (December 1973): 73-88.

   Argues against the guidelines established by the Supreme Court to regulate obscenity, especially the application of contemporary community standards, in *Miller* v. *California*. Since a national standard cannot be determined, a statewide standard must be employed in obscenity cases, if only because the alternative of widely varying local standards is impractical.

156. Mann, Jay; Jack Sidman; and Sheldon Starr. "Evaluating Social Consequences of Erotic Films: An Experimental Approach." *Journal of Social Issues* 29 (1973): 113-131.

   Couples married at least ten years were exposed to erotic and nonerotic films and their subsequent sexual behavior recorded with the use of a checklist on sexual activity over a 12-week period. Films failed to produce sustained changes in frequency or quality of sexual behavior, though short-term increases were observed. Attitudes toward legal dissemination of erotic films grew more liberal.

157. Marcuse, F.L. "Some Reflections on Pornography and Censorship." *Canadian Forum* 54 (March 1975): 13-16.

   Considers general issues involved in the pornography controversy. Does not attempt to distinguish between erotica and pornography, because such distinctions are impractical. Questions the arbitrariness and absurdity of methods used to determine pornography for which censorship is then justified. No current findings demonstrate any relationships between pornography and sexual crimes. Argues against censorship of sex, but suggests censorship of violence might be appropriate.

158. Martin, Jay. "King of Smut: Henry Miller's Tragical History." *Antioch Review* 35 (Fall 1977): 342-367.

   Detailed biographical sketch of Henry Miller and his problems with censorship of several of his novels. The publishing problems of *Tropic of Cancer*, *Tropic of Capricorn*, and *The Crazy Cock* (still unpublished) are detailed. The uncontested publication of *Sexus* in 1964 demonstrated how attitudes toward obscenity had changed.

159. Michelson, Peter. "The Pleasures of Commodity or to Make the World Safe for Pornography." *Antio view* 29 (Spring 1969): 77-90.

    Argues that pornography flourishes because sex is good business. *Playboy* and *Cosmopolitan* are examples of publications that use sex to maximize their profits. Contends that they are successful because they are "slick," i.e. discreet and relatively tasteful. Since both provide instruction while selling sex, they have redeeming social value.

160. Misham, Edward J. "Making the World Safe for Pornography." *Encounter* 38 (March 1972): 9-30.

    Contends that the presence of pornography as a public and open phenomenon reflects the technological and non-religious culture. Examines numerous arguments in defense of easy dissemination of erotica and finds them lacking. Argues that the trend of growing pornography markets will not be reversed without invoking laws which make the purchase of such materials difficult.

161. Molz, Kathleen. "The Public Custody of High Pornography." *American Scholar* 36 (Winter 1966-1967): 93-103.

    An exegesis of the librarian's role in the selection of materials of a controversial sexual nature. Historical background is provided and the influence of contemporary judicial rulings on book selection is discussed. An argument is advanced advocating literary discrimination in lieu of legal abolition.

162. Money, J., and R. Athanasiou. "Pornography--Review and Bibliographic Annotations." *American Journal of Obstetrics and Gynecology* 115 (1973): 130-146.

    Reviews 40 studies concerning obscenity. Reports the following conclusions: (1) no legal definition of obscenity exists; (2) erotic arousal cannot be accurately measured; (3) constant exposure leads to boredom; (4) males and females respond somewhat differently; (5) personal exposure most often occurs in the late 20s to early 30s; (6) political opinions influence personal reactions to pornography; (7) hormonal and chromosomal variation may affect response to erotic materials; (8) availability of pornography may positively affect normal sexual development.

163. Nawy, Harold. "In the Pursuit of Happiness? Consumers
     of Erotica in San Francisco." *Journal of Social
     Issues* 29 (1973): 147-161.

     Patrons of adult bookstores, arcades and movie the-
     aters were observed and asked to respond by question-
     naire. Data suggested that attendance at theaters and
     bookstores is mostly male, and that the average customer
     is white, middle-aged, married, college-educated and
     employed in a white-collar occupation.

164. Peek, Charles W., and Sharon Brown. "Pornography as a
     Political Symbol: Attitudes Toward Commercial Nudity
     and Attitudes Toward Political Organizations." *Social
     Science Quarterly* 58 (March 1978): 717-723.

     Examines the degree to which attitudes toward pornog-
     raphy correlate to other political and social opinions.
     Attitudes toward commercial nudity were found to be con-
     sistently linked to opinions of certain political or-
     ganizations. Negative responses to pornography corre-
     sponded to positive attitudes toward the police, the FBI
     and the United States and a more negative opinion of
     Russia. Concludes that group contexts must be carefully
     considered when investigating the political significance
     of the obscenity issue.

165. Pellak, Felix. "Pornography: A Trip Around the Half-
     world." *Tri-Q* 12 (Spring 1968): 120-138.

     Argues for censorship, but is also in favor of pornog-
     raphy. Without some sort of repression pornography
     will be "obliterated." Continued exposure to and avail-
     ability of pornography will lessen its effect and desir-
     ability. Concludes that attempts to censor pornography
     have the opposite effect: "pruned saplings grow lush."

166. Pilpel, Harriet F., and Marjorie T. Parsons. "Dirty
     Business in Court." *Civil Liberties Review* 1 (Fall)
     1974): 30-41.

     Explores the background of the 1973-1974 Supreme Court
     obscenity decisions, especially in *Miller* v. *California*.
     Difficulties in determining community standards and
     whether a work lacked "serious literary, artistic, po-
     litical, or scientific value" are demonstrated in later
     court cases (*Jenkins* v. *Georgia* and *Hamling* v. *United
     States*). Urges individuals to fight for freedom of ex-
     pression and civil liberties.

167. Ragsdale, J. Donald. *"Last Tango in Paris, et aι. The Supreme Court*: The Current State of Obscenity Lα. *Quarterly Journal of Speech* 61 (October 1975): 279-289.

   Reviews major U.S. Supreme Court decisions since June 1973 and the litigation concerning *Last Tango in Paris*. The tests of obscenity as defined by the Supreme Court (*Miller* v. *California*, 413 U.S. 15, 1973), i.e. serious value test, patent offensiveness test and community standards test, are applied to current litigation, especially those cases involving *Last Tango in Paris* and *The Exorcist*.

168. Reed, John Plume, and Robin S. Reed. "Profile of the Student Censor: A Research Note on Pornography." *Sociological Symposium* 5 (Fall 1970): 53-60.

   Identifies characteristics of potential student censors of obscene materials. 132 sociology students at a medium-sized Southern university responded to erotic pictures and readings. A censoring student is probably a female, married, regular churchgoer, Baptist and with little personal sexual experience. Concludes the student censor is a traditionalist and conservative.

169. Rodgers, Harrell R. "Censorship Campaigns in Eighteen Cities: An Impact Analysis." *American Politics Quarterly* 2 (October 1974): 371-392.

   Analyzes how effective the decisions on obscenity by the Supreme Court have been in protecting both the right of newsdealers to sell and the right of the public to buy certain types of sexually-oriented materials. Concludes that these rights have been protected. Censorship groups are typically ineffective in the long run, even though some initial suppression often occurs. The Supreme Court's increasingly liberal definition of legal publications serves to "thwart" most censorship movements.

170. Rosenfield, Lawrence W. "Politics and Pornography." *Quarterly Journal of Speech* 59 (December 1973): 413-422.

   Employing a rhetorical perspective, author contends that pornography is a form of public address and as such constitutes an effective measure of a person's confidence in his political effectiveness. Various aspects of literary and visual pornography are correlated with

attitudes and impotency and powerlessness on the part
of the consumers of such material. Changes in the quan-
tity or the quality of pornography could indicate a
changing emphasis by society toward political or public
affairs.

171. Rossi, Lee D. "The Whore vs. the Girl-Next-Door: Ste-
      reotypes of Women in *Playboy*, *Penthouse*, and *Oui*."
      Journal of Popular Culture 9 (Summer 1975): 90-94.

      Points out that soft-core pornographic magazines sup-
      port certain aspects of women's liberation (i.e. open
      sexuality), but reject other claims (by women) for so-
      cial and economic equality with men. Contrasts the
      "well-scrubbed sexuality" of *Playboy* with the "decadent
      sexuality" of *Penthouse* and *Oui*. Regardless, however,
      all three magazines are considered to be demeaning and
      are repugnant to the women's movement.

172. Sachs, Walker. "Sex Magazines: No Business Like Show
      Business." *Business and Society Review* (Winter 1976-
      1977): 21-25.

      Examines the expanding market for "adult-sophisticate"
      magazines. Such publications are very lucrative, al-
      though most profits come from sales, as few can attract
      advertisers. *Hustler* is cited as an example of an in-
      creasingly popular type of sex magazine. Such magazines
      are considered a form of entertainment, an adult comic
      book. *Hustler* is labeled the "McDonald's of sex maga-
      zines."

173. Slade, Joseph W. "Pornographic Theaters Off Times
      Square." *Trans-action* 9 (1971): 35-43.

      Describes pornographic theaters, films and viewers
      found in New York's Times Square. Two categories of
      hard-core films are identified: the supposed sexual
      documentary with redeeming social value and the stag
      film. Concludes that pornographic films, like gay lib-
      eration or communal marriages, are simply an example of
      changing sexual attitudes.

174. Slade, Joseph W. "Recent Trends in Pornographic Films."
      Society 12 (1975): 77-84.

      Reviews four pornographic films (*The Hottest Show on
      Earth*, *Defiance*, *French Blue* and *Masters of Discipline*).
      Concludes that with the social acceptance of films such
      as *Deep Throat* producers must resort to "kinkier fanta-

sies." Anal intercourse and fellatio are areas of current interest. Three taboos were discovered--violence against women, excrement and male homosexuality.

175. Smith, Don D. "The Social Content of Pornography." *Journal of Communication* 26 (Winter 1976): 16-24.

428 adult paperbacks were chosen randomly for content analysis between 1967 and 1974. All consisted of explicit sex episodes linked by brief nonsexual portions. A definite increase in the number and length of the sex scenes was noted after 1969. Concludes that plots, themes and stories have remained basically the same. Women's liberation has not affected the extreme male chauvinism typically found in such paperbacks.

176. Smith, LeRoy W. "Daniel Defoe: Incipient Pornographer." *Literature and Psychology* 22 (1972): 165-178.

Points out similarities between two of Daniel Defoe's novels, *Moll Flanders* and *Roxana*, and current hard-core pornography. Similar plot elements, i.e. incestuous relationships, and characters, i.e. highly sexually responsive women, are detailed. Suggests a link between Defoe and libertinism and labels him as a forerunner of hard-core pornography.

177. Sontag, Susan. "The Pornographic Imagination." *Partisan Review* 34 (Spring 1967): 181-214.

Questions whether some pornographic texts possess sufficient artistic merit to be considered "literature." Two examples, *The Story of O* and *The Image*, are examined in detail and concluded to belong to the literary category. Determination of what is pornographic depends on the experience and consciousness of the reader.

178. Stevens, Kenneth R. "*United States* v. *31 Photographs*: Dr. Alfred C. Kinsey and Obscenity Law." *Indiana Magazine of History* 71 (December 1975): 299-318.

Reviews the legal difficulties encountered by Dr. Kinsey and the Institute of Sex Research in importing various examples of erotica. The controversy with the Customs Bureau culminated in *United States* v. *31 Photographs*. This 1957 decision introduced the concept of "variable obscenity," whereby obscenity determination depends on the nature of the intended audience. However, this variable concept has not been accepted as the standard definition for obscenity, and the term remains virtually undefinable.

179. Stewart, Douglas J. "Pornography, Obscenity, and Capi-
      talism." *Antioch Review* 35 (Fall 1977): 389-398.

      Distinguishes between obscenity (anything which happens
      to offend anybody) and pornography (something which
      seeks to arouse sexual passions). Argues that Cleland's
      Fanny Hill is pornographic, although representative of a
      new type. The influence of the Industrial Revolution
      is shown in Cleland's depiction of sex and sex acts as
      commodities or economic acts. Numerous excerpts are
      provided to show this new emphasis on industrial imag-
      ery instead of romantic descriptions.

180. Sumberg, Theodore A. "Privacy, Freedom, and Obscenity:
      Stanley v. *Georgia*." *Journal of Critical Analysis* 3
      (July 1971): 84-96.

      Contends that *Stanley* v. *Georgia* (394 U.S. 565) rep-
      resents a mistake by the Supreme Court. Views the de-
      cision as "soft" and as too protective of the First
      Amendment. Access to pornography, not censorship, re-
      sults in mind control. Not only the Constitution, but
      also the Declaration of Independence, is used to dispute
      the decision.

181. Sundholm, Charles A. "The Pornographic Arcade: Ethno-
      graphic Notes on Moral Men in Immoral Places." *Urban
      Life and Culture* 2 (April 1973): 85-104.

      Examines the five stages of behavioral involvement in
      a pornographic film arcade: (1) entrance; (2) making
      change; (3) looking for a machine; (4) using a machine;
      and (5) exiting. Patrons typically enter alone and en-
      gage in no verbal interaction with other patrons or the
      cashier. Machines located in the rear offer more pri-
      vacy, cost more, and are often used for masturbation,
      an expected and accepted behavior if done privately.

182. Tedford, Thomas L. "What Every Teacher Should Know
      About the Obscenity Decisions." *The Education Digest*
      40 (January 1975): 41-43.

      Provides brief historical account of 20th-century
      court rulings on obscenity focusing on the concepts of
      "clear and present danger," "literary worth" and "pru-
      rient interest." Warns that the 1973 Burger Court rul-
      ings are a serious threat to free speech.

183. Walker, Alexander. "Beyond the Excremental Cinema."
      Encounter 42 (May 1974); 47-52.

Reviews a wide variety of erotic films. Spec
phasis is given to *Last Tango in Paris*, *The Nig*
and *Deep Throat*. Concludes that many current m
whether overtly pornographic or major studio pro
have switched from portraying human relationship   ᴄᴧᴇ
visual presentation of bodily functions--masturbation,
vomiting, urination, etc. Laments this change from emotions to physical functions.

184. Wallace, Douglas H. "Obscenity and Contemporary Community Standards: A Survey." *Journal of Social Issues*
29 (1973): 53-68.

1083 adults were exposed to "response booklets" con-
taining erotic stimuli. Results indicated that no uni-
form standard or criterion was used by the subjects as
they evaluated the items, thus challenging the "single
contemporary community standard" hypothesis.

185. Wallace, Douglas, and Gerald Wehmer. "Evaluation of
Visual Erotica by Sexual Liberals and Conservatives."
Journal of Sex Research 8 (May 1972): 147-153.

Reports a study conducted to obtain some empirical
support for previous theories regarding reaction to pornography by intellectuals and antiintellectuals. The
former, labeled liberals, were more often male, younger
and Jewish. The latter, labeled conservatives, were
older, less educated and less religious. Liberals
viewed pornography more frequently and reacted with sexual arousal. Conservatives reacted with mixed disgust
and arousal. Sexual liberals and conservatives tended
also to be sociopolitical liberals and conservatives.

186. Wheelock, Alan. "The Tarnished Image." *Nursing Outlook*
24 (August 1976): 509-510.

Examines the portrayal of nurses in "sexploitation"
movies. Nurses are presented as promiscuous, stupid and
totally obedient to men. This stereotype results par-
tially from the actual position of nurses in the American health care system. Nurses are typically at the
bottom of the power hierarchy. Three films representing
different genres are discussed: *Not as a Stranger* (1958),
The Blob (1957) and *M*A*S*H** (1970).

187. Wilcoxon, Reba. "Pornography, Obscenity, and Rochester's
'The Imperfect Enjoyment.'" *Studies in English Literature* 15 (Summer 1975): 375-390.

   Examines the poetry of John Wilmot, Earl of Rochester.
   Many of his poems have traditionally been considered
   obscene and frequently have been censored in or deleted
   from editions of his work. Argues that Rochester's
   poems are not pornographic and are worthy of literary
   and aesthetic analysis. "The Imperfect Enjoyment," a
   poem with explicit language and sexual descriptions, is
   studied and shown to present an ethical and moral state-
   ment.

188.   Wilson, James Q. "On Pornography: III--Violence, Pornog-
          raphy, and Social Science." *Public Interest* 22 (Win-
          ter 1971): 45-61.

   Contrasts the findings of the National Commission on
   the Causes and Prevention of Violence and the Commission
   on Obscenity and Pornography. The former concluded that
   violence on television affects the viewer, but the latter
   found no relationship between viewing pornography and
   future actions. Proof of either contention is lacking,
   and this is attributed to the inability of social
   science research to decide an issue that is ultimately
   a moral one.

Here

189.   Wilson, W. Cody. "Facts Versus Fears: Why Should We
          Worry About Pornography." *Annals of the American
          Academy of Political and Social Science* 397 (Septem-
          ber 1971): 105-117.

   Presents data on exposure and behavioral effects of
   pornography with the perspective that many myths have
   grown up regarding the harm such materials create in
   the society. Facts include: (1) a large percentage of
   the population has been exposed; (2) most exposure was
   to activity which conforms to social norms; (3) first
   exposure generally occurs before the age of 18; (4)
   consumers were usually white, middle-aged and middle
   class; and (5) criminals reported less than average
   exposure to erotica in adolescence. Author warns of
   considerable dangers in attempting to repress erotica.

190.   Wilson, W. Cody. "Law Enforcement Officers' Perceptions
          of Pornography as a Social Issue." *Journal of Social
          Issues* 29 (1973): 41-51.

   A mail questionnaire was sent to a random sample of
   district attorneys in the United States. Results indicated that the community problem of obscenity and
   pornography is perceived in a wide variety of ways and

degrees. Concern is highly correlated with city size
and increased availability. Citizenry is viewed generally as apathetic.

191. Wilson, W. Cody. "Pornography: The Emergence of a Social
     Issue and the Beginning of Psychological Study."
     Journal of Social Issues 29 (1973): 7-17.

     Provides brief historical background on the current
     pornography and obscenity debates from a judicial and
     legislative perspective. The author notes that the
     creation of the Commission on Obscenity and Pornography
     in 1967 constituted the first significant impetus to
     gathering empirical data for scientific research into
     pornography and obscenity.

192. Zurcher, Louis A., and J. Kenneth Monts. "Political
     Efficacy, Political Trust, and Anti-Pornography Cru-
     sading: A Research Note." *Sociology and Social Re-
     search* 56 (January 1972): 211-220.

     Discusses the relationship between political efficacy,
     i.e. the ability to influence the political system,
     political trust and participation in antipornography
     organizations. An imbalance with increased political
     efficacy and decreased political trust is associated
     with involvement of citizens in political action against
     pornography. Interviews were conducted with active par-
     ticipants in antipornography crusades in two cities
     identified as Midville and Southtown.

193. Zurcher, Louis A.; R. George Kirkpatrick; Robert Cushing;
     and Charles K. Bowman. "Ad Hoc Antipornography Or-
     ganizations and Their Active Members: A Research
     Summary." *Journal of Social Issues* 29 (1973): 69-94.

     By employing four field techniques (nonparticipant
     observation, document research, informal interview and
     formal interview) natural histories of two antipornog-
     raphy campaigns were assembled and characteristics of
     participants and leaders assessed. Tested the hypoth-
     esis that such campaigns are norm-oriented social
     movements and that leaders and active participants would
     be status discontents.

194. Zurcher, Louis A.; R. George Kirkpatrick; Robert G.
     Cushing; and Charles K. Bowman. "The Anti-Pornog-
     raphy Campaign: A Symbolic Crusade." *Social Problems*
     19 (Fall 1971): 217-238.

Compares two antipornography campaigns conducted in two towns designated Southtown and Midville. Both campaigns are norm-oriented social movements and symbolic crusades. Each also fits the value-added stages of collective behavior. Concludes that most of the results of the antipornography crusades were of more symbolic than utilitarian value.

195. Zurcher, Louis A., Jr., and Russell L. Curtis. "A Comparative Analysis of Propositions Describing Social Movement Organizations." *Sociological Quarterly* 14 (Spring 1973): 175-188.

Studies two antipornography crusades to compare their structure and dynamics to those hypothesized for national, established social-movement organizations. Antipornography movements, since they are oriented toward one specific goal, tend to: (1) be exclusive in membership; (2) have a short duration; (3) be conservative in tactics; (4) resist mergers with other organizations; and (5) be very homogeneous.

IV

PHILOSOPHICAL AND RELIGIOUS ARTICLES

196. Beeson, Trevor. "Pornophobia; The Longford Commission
      Report." *Christian Century* 89 (October 18, 1972):
      1032-1033.

      Refutes numerous conclusions of the Longford Commis-
      sion Report. Since the commission produced no evidence
      indicating that pornography is harmful to either indi-
      viduals or society, its proposed law reforms are un-
      acceptable. Urges that the commission's conclusions be
      very critically considered. Such commissions that cam-
      paign for additional restrictive laws are as dangerous
      as the pornographers themselves.

197. Cleath, Robert L. "Pornography: Purulent Infection."
      Christianity Today 20 (October 10, 1975): 21-22.

      Surveys briefly the evolution of porno films from
      nudist camps to current portrayals of kinky sex acts.
      Worries about general acceptance of such popular movies
      as *Deep Throat*. Concludes that pornography prospers
      because sinners are willing to pay for it. However,
      the open availability of such material is a powerful
      temptation. Therefore, Christians are urged to use le-
      gal means to restrict it.

198. Crossley, D.J. "F.H. Bradley on Censorship and Psychi-
      cal Distance." *Idealistic Studies* 3 (January 1973):
      80-102.

      Discusses an article by F.H. Bradley which deals
      with censorship and aesthetics. Bradley believes in a
      possible causal link between ideas and actions, but
      this is only a tendency, not an absolute. Therefore,
      Bradley does not advocate censorship of literature.
      Psychical distance is presented as a possible solution
      to the problem of censorship. Differences of opinion

regarding pornography result from the distance observers
have from involvement with the material.

199. Dyal, Robert A. "Is Pornography Good for You?" *South-
      western Journal of Philosophy* 7 (Fall 1976): 95-118.

      Argues that the concept cf pornography has been con-
      fused with that of obscenity and that this lack of dif-
      ferentiation is the source of judicial and other dis-
      putes. Analyzes the effects of pornography as a social
      benefit or harm and concludes that all regulation of
      pornographic materials should be ended. Contends pornog-
      raphy is not a matter of public policy, and that pornog-
      raphy should be considered as a type of expression.

200. Fore, W.F. "The Court and Obscenity: Case-by-Case
      Decisions." *Christian Century* 91 (July 17-24, 1974):
      717-718.

      Reviews Supreme Court decisions. Contends that
      Jenkins v. *Georgia*, which concerned the showing of the
      film *Carnal Knowledge*, proves that the earlier decision
      in *Miller* v. *California* is unworkable. The *Carnal
      Knowledge* decision is seen as a victory for the publish-
      ing and motion picture industries. Concludes that ex-
      cept in the case of unsolicited advertising, no govern-
      ment censorship for adults should be allowed in any
      form.

201. Gastil, Raymond D. "The Moral Right of the Majority
      to Restrict Obscenity and Pornography Through Law."
      Ethics 86 (April 1976): 231-240.

      Argues that a majority of citizens has the right to
      regulate obscenity. Contends that a plausible argument
      can be presented that harm results from public pornog-
      raphy. Pornography and obscenity should be regulated
      in the same fashion as littering. All cause public
      harm. The spread of pornography is seen as a victory
      of science over religious beliefs, and arguments for
      its restriction are presented in perfectionist terms
      such as those of Moore, de Jouvenal and Rashdall.

202. Heir, Hilde. "Obscenity, Politics and Pornography."
      Journal of Aesthetic Education 5 (October 1971): 77-97.

      Classifies pornography as obscene and "inherently ob-
      jectionable." Distinguishes between obscenity, which
      simply offends, and pornography, which glorifies per-
      version and inhuman activity. No conclusion is reached

regarding the restriction of pornography. Societal attitudes toward sex and women are deeply ingrained and
difficult to change. Urges further intelligent study
of this problem.

203. Hunnex, Milton. "Sex Profiteering and the Evangelical."
     Christianity Today 19 (June 6, 1975): 16-20.

     Argues that: (1) we do know what is obscene and what
     isn't; (2) though the possibility of abuse through cen-
     sorship is present, we must restrict access to erotica;
     (3) access to materials must be restricted for adults
     as well as children; (4) pornography dehumanizes sex;
     (5) pornography influences attitudes and behavior; and
     (6) profiteering in obscenity must be ended.

204. Jacobson, Beverly. "A Bookstore Perishes: How an Ob-
     scenity Law Victimized a Respectable Business Woman."
     Christian Century 91 (October 23, 1974): 990-992.

     Reports the case of Carole Grant, the owner of the
     only bookstore in Orem, Utah, who was forced out of
     business following a lengthy legal battle over her al-
     leged selling of obscene materials. The obscenity leg-
     islation in Orem was very specific and offered a bounty
     for complaints that resulted in conviction. Several
     major publishers provided legal assistance, and an out-
     of-court settlement was reached which resulted in the
     dropping of all charges. However, Mrs. Grant closed
     the bookstore.

205. Jarrett, James L. "On Pornography." *Journal of Aes-
     thetic Education* 4 (July 1970): 61-68.

     Reviews various definitions of and criteria for pornog-
     raphy. Points out that the term "pornography" is
     usually used pejoratively and is broadly applied to ex-
     plicit sexual materials. A neutral, valueless connota-
     tion may allow the material so designated to be judged
     more objectively. There could be exciting, well-written
     pornography and boring poorly written pornographic ma-
     terials. Certain pornographic works could then be
     morally censured, if not legally censored.

206. Johnson, Dick. "Pornography Decision Infringes on
     Constitutional Guarantees." *Engage/Social Action* 1
     (September 1973): 51-53.

     Contends that the 1973 Supreme Court decisions are not
     an appropriate way to handle the problem of pornography.

Christians must be concerned about the increasing deg-
radation represented by pornography, but they must be
wary of infringing on the First Amendment rights of
others in trying to censor pornographic materials. Like
prohibition, regulations on pornography will not result
in suppression or elimination of such materials.

207. Kaelin, E.F. "The Pornographic and the Obscene in Legal and Aesthetic Contexts." *Journal of Aesthetic
Education* 4 (July 1970): 69-84.

Contends that courts must rely on broader aesthetic
judgments when determining obscenity. A judgment on
only subject matter is insufficient. The entire work
must be considered. Intent and effect are irrelevant.
It is theoretically possible to determine pornography
through aesthetic analysis. Reviews and cites many
articles.

208. Kuhn, Harold B. "The 'Right to Leer.'" *Christianity
Today* 21 (November 5, 1976): 89-90.

Argues that an evangelical approach to erotica must
concern itself with moral and spiritual values. Such
material constitutes a demeaning of the inner person,
which is vulnerable to moral corruption, and requires
regulation as a spiritual protection.

209. Oboler, Eli. "'Just Like the Child in the Family':
Paternalistic Morality and Censorship." *Library
Journal* 98 (September 1, 1973): 2395-2398.

Employs the philosophical distinctions of private and
public morality to analyze the desirability of censorship regarding pornographic materials. Argues that
such censorship constitutes paternalism and requires
clear evidence of harm to those being protected before
censorship should be imposed.

210. "Outer Limits of Free Speech." *Christian Century* 90
(May 2, 1973): 499-500.

Discusses the section on obscenity that is to be included in the proposed revision of the U.S. Criminal
Code. Although it is hard for a religious publication
to oppose a statute designed to eliminate hard-core
pornography, this editorial argues against this legislation. Free speech is too important to democracy to
be limited in an attempt to control pornography. Also,
the dangers of pornography to adults have not been docu-
mented.

211. "Pornography and Court Presuppositions." *Christian Century* 90 (July 18-25, 1973): 747-748.

     Reacts to the several obscenity decisions handed down by the Supreme Court in June 1973. Argues that local standards are not appropriate in a "pluralistic and highly mobile society." Although children should be protected from pornography and such materials should not be publicly displayed in an offensive fashion, this editorial concludes that further restrictions interfere with free speech. The adult marketplace may eventually lose its interest in pornography.

212. Regan, John J. "The Obscenity Problem: Time for a Truce?" *Catholic World* 207 (April 1968): 70-73.

     Reviews the decisions in recent court cases, including *Roth*, *Fanny Hill*, *Redrup* and *Ginzburg* and discusses the criteria laid down by the courts for defining obscene materials. Contends that legal battles are unproductive and that more energy should be directed to educating individuals as morally responsible persons.

213. Rodes, Robert E., Jr. "Baneful Business Enterprise: Moral Choices in Contemporary Society." *National Catholic Reporter* 13 (April 1, 1977): 8.

     Attempts to refute the basic arguments for the free dissemination of pornographic materials. Contends that pornography is not art, does not liberate an individual sexually and does not possess an idea which would protect it legally. Recommends activism on the part of religious groups so that enforcement of present laws is consistent.

214. Schalk, Adolph. "Pornography: Not so Rotten in Denmark." *U.S. Catholic/Jubilee* 36 (February 1971): 32-38.

     Reports how Denmark has reacted to the legalization of pornography. Offers four conclusions: (1) pornography is relatively hard to find in Denmark; (2) pornography is very, very boring; (3) legalizing pornography is not necessarily harmful; and (4) pornography is only one problem, out of many. The drug problem is the main problem in Denmark. Few Danes are opposed to the liberalization of obscenity laws.

215. Sisk, John P. "Pornography: Shameless or Revolutionary: Moral Choices in Contemporary Society." *National Catholic Reporter* 13 (April 1, 1977): 8.

Examines the argument that pornography is an important
aspect of revolution in that it counters attempts to
suppress the human spirit. Questions whether the concept of shame is a valuable one in regard to pornography
and whether its elimination would, in fact, create a
healthier attitude toward sexuality. Compares present
social attitudes to those surrounding *Huckleberry Finn*.

216. Smith, Thomas J. "How to Ban a Dirty Book." *U.S.
      Catholic* 41 (August 1976): 13-14.

Urges local control of adult bookstores, theaters and
entertainment establishments. Points out that liquor
and zoning laws are accepted and that gambling and pros-
titution are legally prohibited. Contends that local
communities should simply, but explicitly, legislate
their desires with regard to obscenity. Arguments that
local control of pornography will result in censorship
of Shakespeare will be proven unfounded. Americans have
the legal right to control pornography locally.

217. Stuart, I.R. "Personality Dynamics and Objectionable
      Art: Attitudes, Opinions, and Experimental Evidence."
      Journal of Aesthetic Education 4 (July 1970): 101-116.

Contends that pornography is concerned only with the
external sex act and, consequently, cannot be related
to aesthetics, which demands inherent value. Any work
that claims to be art must deal with more than a narrow
obsession with sexual activity. Students of aesthetics
must be taught to distinguish between art (intrinsic
value) and pornography (no inherent value).

218. Taylor, Mark. "Censorship or Pornography?" *Commonweal*
      99 (December 7, 1973): 260-264.

Contends that the main enemy of freedom of expression
is pornography, not censorship. Pornography dehumanizes
sex and treats human beings as beasts or machines. The
inevitable result of such attitudes is a totalitarian
mentality. Pornography must be censored if freedom of
expression is to be guaranteed.

219. Tischler, N.M. "Pious Pornography." *Christianity
      Today* 15 (April 23, 1971): 14-15.

Defines "pious pornography" as the use in a story of
a central religious figure to whom is attributed "ex-
aggerated sexuality." Sinclair Lewis's *Elmer Gantry*
and John Updike's *Couples* are cited as examples, as are

the novels of William Styron. This combination of
religious attributes and sexual activities is confusing
to the reader. Pious pornography is judged to be worse
than blatant hard-core pornography which can be readily
identified.

220. Wall, James M. "Matter of Taste." *Christian Century*
92 (April 30, 1975): 427-428.

Distinguishes between being repelled by an individual's taste in reading or viewing material and controlling that individual's taste. Religious leaders must
resist their desire to lead censorship campaigns against
pornography. Contends that such censorship is self-de-
feating and has no place in a democracy.

221. Wall, James M. "Two Payments for Freedom." *Christian
Century* 93 (July 7-14, 1976): 619.

Analyzes the Supreme Court's decision to allow cities
to restrict "adult" bookstores and movies to certain
areas. The Court apparently has concluded that there
are limits to how far commercial sex can be exploited.
This editorial believes that restricting the location
of pornography is a reasonable price to pay for assur-
ing continued freedom of expression in all areas.

222. White, David A. "Censorship and the Concept of Imitation." *New Scholasticism* 48 (Autumn 1974): 464-480.

Evaluates the opinion that censorship is objectionable
because most people are inadequately educated as far as
being able to determine the artistic value of poten-
tially censurable works. The concept of imitation and
its relationship to plot as present in Aristotle's
Poetics is used to consider possible justifications for
censorship. If Aristotle's theory that imitations are
intrinsically pleasurable is accepted, a theoretical
rationale for censorship can be established. In an
ideal world no censorship would be necessary, because
all men would be properly educated.

223. Williston, Frank S. "A Philosophic Analysis of Pornography." *Journal of Thought* 7 (April 1972): 95-105.

Contends that pornography is a social event that is
relevant to philosophy. Pornography is a "personal
idiom for dealing with social taboos." Since fantasies
are involved, epistemological concepts can be considered.
Concludes that a philosophical analysis of obscenity

illustrates the failure of dialectic humanism to solve
the problems involved in synthesizing rationalism and
empiricism.

224. Winthrop, Henry. "Dialectic and the Collective Judicial
     Definition of the Obscene." *Religious Humanism* 9
     (Summer 1975): 108-114.

     Addresses the definition of obscenity as determined
     in the courts, primarily the Supreme Court. Argues that
     this collective, judicial definition is "worthless."
     Ambiguities and vague abstractions are criticized. Sug-
     gestions are given to improve the courts' definition. A
     group of lay judges might be used to analyze the con-
     tents to determine "prurient interest." Any new defini-
     tion of pornography must consider psychological, socio-
     logical, anthropological and aesthetic factors.

225. Zimmer, Steven L. "How One Southern City Faced the Ob-
     scenity Standards Issue." *Christian Century* 91 (Sep-
     tember 25, 1974): 884-886.

     Reports the activities of the Jefferson County (Ken-
     tucky) Commission on Community Standards Related to Ob-
     scenity. Established in response to *Miller* v. *Cali-
     fornia*, the commission solicited community involvement
     to determine local standards. Few individuals or groups
     responded, and public hearings were poorly attended.
     Lack of public response was attributed to distrust in
     government and little understanding of obscenity laws.
     While pornography had few proponents, no substantial
     objection to it was evident.

V

POPULAR ARTICLES

226. Andrist, Ralph K. "Paladin of Purity." *American Heri-
     tage*, October 1973, p. 4.

     Brief history of Anthony Comstock, 19th-century cru-
     sader against pornography and other vices. Discussion
     of moral and political forces at work during his life
     and a perspective on his rise and later diminution of
     power.

227. Barrett, James K. "Inside the Mob's Smut Rackets."
     Reader's Digest, November 1973, pp. 128-132.

     Ex-Mafia member recounts experiences as a dealer in
     erotica in Baltimore. Contends pornography industry is
     Mafia-dominated with pay-offs and other illegal activ-
     ities closely associated with it. Discusses in partic-
     ular peep shows, strippers and stag films.

228. Bender, Paul. "The Obscenity Muddle." *Harper's Magazine*,
     February 1973, pp. 46-52.

     Traces the decisions of 20th-century Supreme Court on
     the issue of obscenity and notes that the criteria
     established by the Roth decision only served to confuse
     the important issues. Argues that any decision should
     take into account the various types of pornography and
     to whom the pornography is disseminated.

229. Blake, Richard A. "Will Fig Leaves Blossom Again?"
     America, August 18, 1973, pp. 82-84.

     Analyzes reaction to recent Supreme Court decisions.
     Two major problems are identified: (1) how will "commu-
     nity standards" be decided? and (2) how can alleged
     pornographic materials be judged for "serious merit"?
     Good state laws and judicial decisions might result in
     success; however, both problems remain unresolved.

230. Blount, Winton M. "Let's Put the Smut Merchants Out of
      Business." *Nation's Business*, September 1971, pp. 34-
      39.

      Postmaster General discusses the growth of pornography
      particularly as it relates to the use of mail and customs
      activity. Contends that erotica is a violation of human
      dignity and a symptom of decadence. Argues that the
      First Amendment protection is not absolute and that
      pornography activity must be considered a large business
      whose profits must be reduced through legal restraint.

231. Bretnor, Reginald. "A Plea for Censorship." *Modern
      Age*, Winter 1966/67, pp. 35-44.

      Argues for a "sane censorship" which would limit right
      of the mass media and popular mass movements to produce
      and distribute pornography. Such censorship would ac-
      tually restore and insure personal freedom of speech for
      individuals. Argues that freedom of speech as guaranteed
      by the Constitution is not absolute and can be limited by
      laws.

232. Bridge, Peter. "What Parents Should Know and Do About
      'Kiddie Porn.'" *Parents' Magazine*, January 1978, p.
      42.

      Attempts to acquaint parents with the rise of porno-
      graphic materials using children as subjects. Notes
      that runaways are frequently victims of child pornog-
      raphers, and that this type of erotica ought to be
      viewed as a form of child abuse. Recommends stronger
      federal and state laws, and greater attention to outlets
      of this material.

233. Brothers, Joyce. "What Women Think of Pornography."
      Good Housekeeping, May 1970, pp. 54-55.

      Speculation on why women are not attracted to pornog-
      raphy in the same way men are. Contends sexual activity
      is more arousing for women when conjoined with romance
      or loving relationships. Notes a growing interest by
      women in the male body and attributes this to increases
      in extroversion and aggressiveness. Includes eight-
      question test on facts about pornography.

234. Buckley, Tom. "Oh! Copenhagen." *New York Times Magazine*,
      February 8, 1970, pp. 32-46.

Describes in a wide-ranging fashion the social condi-
tions relating to sexual attitudes and behavior in Denmark following the significant liberalization of pornography laws. Politicians, psychiatrists, professors and
other professionals contribute their views of the society.
Contends that Danish culture is healthy and progressive.

235. "Child's Garden of Perversity." *Time*, April 4, 1977,
      pp. 55-56.

      Discusses the explosion of child pornography in the
      United States. Notes that children are often victims
      of incest, and proponents of stronger laws against such
      material view the use of children as a form of child
      abuse. Using this approach, a clash with First Amend-
      ment rights may be avoided.

236. Christenson, Reo M. "Dealing with Pornography: A Cultural
      or Civil Liberties Problem? A Case for Censorship."
      Current, November 1970, pp. 31-38.

      Argues for stricter regulations concerning distribu-
      tion of pornographic materials. Asserts that sexual
      restraints are a sign of healthy cultures and that the
      First Amendment protections are not absolute. Sugges-
      tions for revisions of Supreme Court decisions are
      offered.

237. Cook, James. "The X-Rated Economy." *Forbes*, September
      18, 1978, pp. 81-92.

      Discussion of the commercial marketing of pornographic
      materials. Notes that as legal and community standards
      are relaxed, mass marketing becomes more and more prof-
      itable. Explores pornography's movement into new media
      such as video cassettes and analyzes the practices of
      leading business competitors in the field. Mentions some
      producers' connections with organized crime.

238. Denison, George. "Pornography, Censorship and Common
      Sense." *Reader's Digest*, February 1974, pp. 115-118.

      Interviews Alexander M. Bickel, Law Professor at Yale,
      on recent court rulings and how they apply to distribu-
      tion of erotica. Contends that local communities can
      now determine what is meant by "prurient interest" and
      "patently offensive," but the courts determine what a
      "serious work" is.

239. Denison, George. "Sultan of Smut." *Reader's Digest*,
      November 1975, pp. 105-109.

      Discusses the rise of Michael George Thevis, who the
      author designates the "Sultan of Smut." Provides a
      brief biography and history of his rise to power not
      only in the pornography business but also in more legit-
      imate enterprises. Connections with organized crime
      are revealed and assertions that Thevis has reformed his
      life are challenged.

240. Densen-Gerber, Judianne. "What Pornographers Are Doing
      to Children: A Shocking Report." *Redbook*, August 1977,
      pp. 86-90.

      Argues that people must take action against child
      pornography. Contends that this form of erotica is a
      form of child abuse and that legislative remedies must
      be sought. Proposes three-pronged legislation requiring
      that: (1) all sex education media be licensed; (2)
      existing statutes be strengthened; and (3) the presence
      of venereal disease be made a *prima facie* proof of child
      abuse.

241. Dudar, Helen. "America Discovers Child Pornography."
      Ms., August 1977, p. 45.

      Discusses the nationwide movements against child
      pornography, with particular attention to the Odyssey
      Institute's attempts to awaken the citizenry to the
      problem. Observes that the average user is a white,
      middle-class male, and that the children are often run-
      aways, prostitutes and drug users. Argues that child
      pornography should be seen as another form of child
      abuse.

242. Engel, A.D. "Dealing with Pornography: A Cultural or
      Civil Liberties Problem? A Case Against Censorship."
      Current, November 1970, pp. 38-43.

      Refutes Reo Christenson's article in the same issue.
      Argues that the motive of the producer of erotica (e.g.
      entertainment or education) cannot be used as a criterion
      for determining whether that material can be censored.
      Asserts that no causal links can be found between erotica
      and antisocial behavior, and that attempts at censorship
      increase our frustrations and the profits of pornographers.

243.   Fahringer, Herald Price. "Censorship and Pornography."
        Humanist, July/August 1977, pp. 30-33.

        Asserts in an interview that recent Supreme Court cases
        have seriously threatened First Amendment rights. Dis-
        cusses the Roth decision, *Deep Throat*, *Hustler* and Al
        Goldstein. Argues that juries and courts should not be
        deciding matters of taste.

244.   Frank, Elizabeth Pope. "What Are They Doing to Our
        Children." *Good Housekeeping*, August 1977, p. 99.

        Discusses the motion picture industry's use of chil-
        dren and sex in movies not usually considered porno-
        graphic. Linda Blair and Jodie Foster are specifically
        treated. Questions whether it is healthy for children to
        view sexual scenes involving other children.

245.   Friedman, Mel. "The Supreme Court and 'Obscenity.'"
        The Nation, August 6, 1977, pp. 110-112.

        Reviews court cases involving obscenity since 1973
        Miller v. *California* ruling. Includes discussion of
        Marks v. *United States*, *Smith* v. *United States*, *Splawn*
        v. *California* and *Ward* v. *Illinois*. Contends that First
        Amendment freedoms are being seriously eroded.

246.   Goodman, Walter. "The Coming of Bold Pornography."
        Current, February 1977, pp. 32-38.

        Interviews conducted by Goodman with author Gay Talese
        and psychoanalyst Ernest van den Haag. Issues center
        around the pros and cons of censorship. Includes dis-
        cussion on defining obscenity and the role that law and
        juries play in adjudicating prosecutions of pornographers.

247.   Greer, Gordon. "Pornography: What Can We Do to Protect
        Our Kids?" *Better Homes and Gardens*, December 1971,
        p. 16.

        Argues briefly that the key problem is not dissemina-
        tion of erotica to adults but how to prevent children
        from exposure. Advocates political pressure and partici-
        pation in civic groups such as churches, clubs and PTA.
        Regards total censorship as ineffective and submits that
        there is no substitute for providing good sex education
        and a loving family as a deterrent to pornography's
        effects.

248. Hanson, Wallace. "Pornography for the People." *Popular
      Photography*, February 1972, pp. 77-79.

      Contends that pornography as a photographic art form
      is seriously hampered in the United States both by seri-
      ous legal penalties and judicial ambiguity. The Roth
      decision and *Memoirs* v. *Massachusetts* are discussed
      briefly as they relate to establishing a criterion for
      assessing pornographic materials.

249. Heiman, J.R. "Women's Sexual Arousal: The Physiology
      of Erotica." *Psychology Today*, April 1975, pp. 90-94.

      Studies women's reaction to and arousal by erotica.
      Women like erotica as much as men and are turned on by
      sexual descriptions. A penile strain gauge and a photo-
      plethysmograph were used to measure arousal in men and
      women. Explicit sex, not romance, was found to be what
      aroused both sexes. Women were most aroused by an
      erotic tape which depicted a female-initiated, female-
      centered story. Concludes that women may be slower to
      admit arousal than men.

250. Judson, Horace Freeland. "Skindeep: How to Watch a
      Pornographic Movie." *Harper's Magazine*, February
      1975, pp. 42-49.

      Probes into the aspects of pornography that could
      make it more of an art form. Books are compared with
      movies with the perspective that movies have failed to
      explore the social and psychological aspect of sex--an
      area that the author designates as "erotic realism."
      Ends with a plea for quality filmmakers and actors to
      enter the pornography area.

251. Kauffmann, Stanley. "Stanley Kauffmann on Obscenity."
      New Republic, October 17, 1970, p. 22.

      Reviews briefly the findings of the Commission on
      Obscenity and Pornography, and argues that laws restrict-
      ing erotica are socially unhelpful. Contends that social
      progress will ultimately render pornography undesirable
      and unnecessary.

252. Keating, Charles H, Jr., "Green Light to Combat Smut."
      Reader's Digest, January 1974, pp. 147-150.

      Argues that the 1973 Burger Court decisions on re-
      striction of pornographic materials constitute a legal
      basis for censoring hard-core erotica. Recommends that

community members report presence of pornography in
stores to local authorities and urge prosecution of
businesses selling such materials.

253. Keating, Charles H., Jr. "The Report That Shocked the
     Nation." *Reader's Digest*, January 1971, pp. 37-41.

     A former member of the Commission on Obscenity and
     Pornography argues that the majority report was biased
     and the scientific experiments poorly conducted. Rec-
     ommends: (1) that individuals act on the local level to
     eliminate pornography dissemination; and (2) that laws
     be enacted that will prevent the Supreme Court from
     reversing obscenity convictions.

254. "Keeping a Rein on Sex Businesses." *Changing Times*,
     January 1978, pp. 21-23.

     Deals primarily with techniques for regulating porno-
     graphic businesses. Two methods are discussed in detail:
     (1) concentrating the businesses in small areas, such as
     the "Combat Zone" in Boston; and (2) dispersing the
     businesses and keeping them away from residences. Both
     employ zoning ordinances for this means.

255. Kirkendall, Lester; Gina Allen; Albert Ellis; and Helen
     Colton. "Sex Magazines and Feminism." *Humanist*,
     November-December 1978, pp. 44-51.

     The authors argue in a symposium that pornography must
     be accepted as a part of human life and that authorities
     in sexual matters must disseminate their knowledge through
     popular magazines, even pornographic ones, to reach the
     relevant audience. Notes that pornography can be life-
     affirming and is not necessarily something demeaning.

256. Kristol, Irving. "Pornography, Obscenity and the Case
     for Censorship." *New York Times Magazine*, March 28,
     1971, p. 24.

     Analyzes pornography in relation to American political,
     social and cultural values. Discusses the basic argu-
     ments against censorship and the ways in which they fail
     to take into account the real issue. Argues that pornog-
     raphy is essentially a dehumanizing phenomenon which
     impoverishes the civilization. Recommends that erotica
     be forced into an "under the counter" condition.

257. Kuh, Richard H. "Obscenity, Censorship, and the Non-
     doctrinaire Liberal." *Wilson Library Bulletin*, May
     1968, pp. 902-909.

Discusses the appropriateness of censorship, particularly in a liberal society. Argues that censorship of pornography is justifiable in regard to distribution to children, in areas of public display and in cases of extreme hard-core pornography. Analysis includes case law and suggestions regarding legislation.

258. Lewin, Nathan. "Sex at High Noon in Times Square." *New Republic*, July 7 and 14, 1973, pp. 19-21.

Analyzes the 1973 Burger Court decisions on erotic materials. Contends that a significant change in interpretation has occurred giving local communities greater power, and that stricter enforcement may create self-censorship on the part of creative artists.

259. McCormick, Kenneth D., and W.L. Smith. "The Guardians of Virtue Mount a New Offensive." *Saturday Review*, July 22, 1972, pp. 24-25.

Discusses the rise of antipornography organizations, including: (1) Citizens for Decent Literature and (2) Morality in Media, and their efforts at censorship. Warns that newspapers and other media are not recognizing the threat of self-censorship or externally imposed restraints. Recommends that groups be developed to oppose antipornography organizations and crusaders.

260. McMurtry, Larry. "From Mickey Spillane to Erica Jong." *Washington Monthly*, May 1975, pp. 12-20.

Reviews the changes in erotic literature since the late 1940s. American sex habits have become more public and very impersonal. Contends that an overemphasis on the mechanics of love has lowered its emotional value. Sexual activity is no longer related to personal character, either in erotic books or in life.

261. Mead, Margaret. "Can We Protect Children from Pornography." *Redbook*, March 1972, pp. 74-80.

Argues that minimal control over pornographic materials is essential, particularly in regard to control of exposure to children. Children, especially those under 12 years old, require protection because they have not fully formed their sexual attitudes and values. Recommends liberal sex education and group actions to oversee distribution of erotica at bookstores.

262. Mead, Margaret. "Women and the 'New' Pornography."
      Redbook, February 1976, pp. 29-32.

      Examines the question of the desirability of pornography
      as its availability increases with the growth of soft-
      core pornography for women. Argues that the liberation
      of women has led to new sexual attitudes, and has had
      a negative effect with regard to pornography. Asserts
      that women have entered into the traditionally male
      domains of vulgarity and sexual exploitation.

263. Michelson, Peter. "The Way the Wind Blows." *The Nation*,
      February 4, 1978, pp. 105-108.

      Discusses the legal ambiguities in the *Miller* v.
      California decision of 1973, and how the case applies to
      the prosecution of current cases. Contends that new
      state laws are caught in cross fire between control of
      obscenity and free speech.

264. Molz, Kathleen. "A Panel Discussion on Censorship and
      Pornography." *Wilson Library Bulletin*, May 1968, pp.
      926-929.

      Provides a general account of the issues raised in a
      panel discussion on pornography and obscenity at the
      New School for Social Research in New York City. Panel
      members are identified and their views summarized.
      Author concludes that the discussion raised a few key
      points but failed to resolve them.

265. Morgan, Ted. "United States Versus the Princes of Porn."
      New York Times Magazine, March 6, 1977, p. 16.

      Discussion of the recent prosecutions of Harry Reems
      and Al Goldstein in light of the *Miller* v. *California*
      decision. Presents the points of view of principals,
      including Larry Parrish, prosecuting attorney. Focuses
      on the issue of prosecuting individuals in conservative
      regions of the country far from the site of production.

266. Murray, William. "The Porn Capitol of America." *New
      York Times Magazine*, January 3, 1971, p. 8.

      Describes the plethora of pornographic offerings in San
      Francisco, including clubs and movie theaters. Dis-
      cusses the antipornography forces and interviews indi-
      viduals involved in the dissemination of erotica. Con-
      siders San Francisco to be the most liberal city in re-
      gard to pornography in the United States.

267. North, Gary. "Pornography, Community, Law." *National
      Review*, August 31, 1973, pp. 943-944.

      Discusses the significance of the Roth decision and
      argues that the Court was correct in giving local com-
      munities the power to decide what should be censored in
      their localities. Believes that erotica is a threat to
      the family structure and to liberal society as a whole.

268. Packer, Herbert L. "The Pornography Caper." *Commentary*,
      February 1971, pp. 72-77.

      Critically analyzes the methods and findings of the
      Commission on Obscenity and Pornography and the response
      of dissenters. Finds too much emphasis on faulty social
      science data and irrational reponses on the part of dis-
      senters. Recommends that First Amendment approaches be
      dropped in favor of the notion of "substantive due pro-
      cess."

269. Pechter, William S. "Deep Tango." *Commentary*, July
      1973, pp. 64-66.

      Reviews *Last Tango in Paris* from the overall perspec-
      tive of the purpose of pornography in film. Contends
      that pornography represents an authentic emotion, par-
      ticularly in regard to the presentation of male ejacula-
      tion. Questions whether pornographic films should be-
      come "art" films, and exposes similarities and differ-
      ences between *Last Tango* and erotica.

270. Pilpel, Harriet F. "Obscenity and the Constitution."
      Publishers Weekly, December 10, 1973, pp. 24-27.

      Suggests ways to react to the 1973 Supreme Court de-
      cisions. Publishers and librarians must fight against
      the restrictions posed by these new obscenity standards.
      Attacks should be made on the constitutionality of most
      obscenity laws. Concludes there should be no obscenity
      laws directed against sex at all. Condensed version
      of Bowker Memorial Lecture on Book Publishing.

271. "The Porn Fighters." *Newsweek*, December 9, 1974, pp.
      74-79.

      Reports on the creation of the National Legal Data
      Center, which is helping prosecutors litigate cases
      against pornographers who retain highly trained defense
      lawyers.

272. "The Porno Plague." *Newsweek*, April 5, 1976, pp. 58-
     63.

     Examines in a wide-ranging fashion the expanding por-
     nography market. Interviews with producers of pornog-
     raphy are included, along with philosophical speculation
     on erotica as a reflection of society. Problems of law
     enforcement and participation of organized crime are
     noted along with discussions of relevant court cases and
     findings of the Commission on Obscenity and Pornography.

273. "Pornography Goes Public." *Newsweek*, December 21, 1970,
     pp. 26-32.

     Discusses the growth of pornography as a business
     throughout the United States. Bookstores, theaters and
     live shows are included in the review. Examines the
     attitudes of law enforcement officers and the significance
     of court cases such as *Fanny Hill* and *Stanley* v. *Georgia*.

274. Rembar, Charles. "Obscenity and the Constitution: A
     Different Opinion." *Publishers Weekly*, January 14,
     1974, pp. 77-79.

     Reacts to Harriet Pilpel's Bowker Memorial Lecture on
     Book Publishing. Contends that she, like many civil
     libertarians, is too pessimistic about the 1973 Supreme
     Court decisions. Such emotional lectures contribute to
     an "unwarranted anxiety." Worries that this anxiety
     will affect not only how authors write, but also how the
     Supreme Court will decide future cases. Concludes that
     even with the current decisions, there is still more
     than enough literary freedom in the United States.

275. Rembar, Charles. "Obscenity--Forget It." *The Atlantic
     Monthly*, May 1977, pp. 37-41.

     Argues that restrictions on erotica should not stem
     from the concept of obscenity, which is fraught with
     ambiguities. Recommends that clear legal concepts should
     be used in the three areas of: (1) protection of children;
     (2) the exposure of erotica to unwilling audiences; and
     (3) sexual behavior.

276. Remsberg, Charles, and Bonnie Remsberg. "Dirty Movies!
     Dirty Books!" *Good Housekeeping*, March 1977, p. 103.

     A review of the activities and philosophy of Larry
     Parrish, Assistant U.S. Attorney in Memphis, Tennessee,
     and active antipornography prosecutor. Offers advice

to citizens on stopping the dissemination of erotica and
claims that in 2 years, the pornography business could
be reduced to the level of 20 years ago.

277. Robbe-Grillet, Alain. "For a Voluptuous Tomorrow."
      Trans. Richard Howard. *Saturday Review*, May 20, 1972,
      pp. 44-46.

      Provides a European literary perspective on pornography
      in New York. Argues that even hard-core erotica makes
      us think about ourselves and use our imaginations, but
      rejects as wholly unfounded the view that such material
      leads to sex offenses.

278. Sagarin, Edward. "On Banning the Beautiful and Showing
      the Ugly." *Humanist*, March 1974, pp. 22-25.

      Claims that the Supreme Court in the Miller decision
      further "muddled" the obscenity situation. Although
      viable reasons can be presented to justify community
      control, such local standards will not work. Hard-core
      pornography will continue to be produced, but serious
      filmmakers will fear local restrictions. Consequently,
      pornography will prosper, but serious erotic art will
      be effectively censored.

279. See, Carolyn. "My Daddy, the Pornographer." *Esquire*,
      August 1972, pp. 110-113.

      Literary reminiscences of her father's prolific output
      of pornographic novels. Discusses a series of her father's
      works with attention to the types of things mentioned
      and the attitudes and values of the characters.

280. Shultz, Gladys Denny. "What Sex Offenders Say About
      Pornography." *Reader's Digest*, July 1971, pp. 53-57.

      Contends that a major conclusion of the Commission on
      Obscenity and Pornography, that erotica has no effect on
      sex crimes, is incorrect. Interviews with sex offenders
      at Waupun Prison in Wisconsin were conducted on an in-
      formal basis and some criminals indicated that they were
      stimulated to commit crimes by exposure to erotica.
      Recommends caution in reducing restrictions on porno-
      graphic materials.

281. Serebnick, Judith. "The 1973 Burger Court Rulings on
      Obscenity: Have They Made a Difference." *Wilson
      Library Bulletin*, December 1975, pp. 304-310.

Discusses the results of a study conducted at ten
medium-size libraries with 210 librarians regarding the
effect that the 1973 Burger Court rulings had on library
practice and policy. Concludes that librarians are aware
of the decisions and often exercise self-imposed restraints on materials. Fears that such cautiousness is
a possible repetition of library activities during the
period of Un-American Activities committees.

282. "Sexploitation: Sin's Wages." *Newsweek*, February 12,
1973, pp. 78-80.

Discusses some of the owners of large pornographic
businesses in the United States. Provides dollar figures
for earnings from production and distribution of erotica.
Contends that proliferation of erotica will not end in
the near future.

283. Smith, Margaret Chase. "Why Women Must Speak Out Against
Pornography." *Reader's Digest*, October 1972, pp. 235-
240.

Laments the growth of pornographic establishments in
the United States, focusing heavily on Southern California as the center for production and distribution.
Recommends that women should: (1) follow developments
in their own community; (2) contact government officials
and ask that tougher antipornography laws be enacted;
and (3) pressure local officials to act to the full
extent of the law.

284. "Smut, Pornography, Obscenity--Signs the Tide is Turning."
U.S. News and World Report, May 7, 1973, pp. 39-44.

Describes the attempts of various cities and organizations to curb the increasing dissemination of pornographic
materials in the United States. Actions by police, the
U.S. Postal Service and citizens' groups in major cities
are discussed. Observes that the struggle against pornography has a long way to go.

285. Sobran, M.J., Jr. "I Say Lock 'Em Up, Spank Them and
Send Them Home." *National Review*, June 24, 1977, p.
712.

Analyzes the philosophical, political and legal concepts of free speech as they pertain to new obscenity
cases. Argues that free speech and First Amendment
rights must be seen in a historical light, and that free
speech does not protect materials that local communities
consider obscene.

286.   Sparrow, John. "Freedom of Expression: Too Much of a
           Good Thing." *American Scholar*, Spring 1977, pp. 165-
           180.

        Argues that free speech and expression should be regu-
        lated by "the requirements of public decency." Analyzes
        three basic and standard arguments against restrictive
        laws regarding obscenity and offers counterarguments.
        Contends that gross violations of human sensibilities
        constitute legitimate grounds for prescription of ob-
        scene materials.

287.   Whelan, Charles M. "Behind the Fig Leaf: A Legal Anal-
           ysis." *America*, August 18, 1973, pp. 84-87.

        Reviews eight principal obscenity cases decided by the
        Supreme Court in 1973. All decisions reaffirm the tra-
        ditional concept that government can regulate and suppress
        obscene materials. The three tests for obscenity are
        discussed and labeled: SWAP ("Sex--Whole Work--Appeal
        to Prurient Interest"); POW ("Patently Offensive Way");
        and SLAPS ("Serious--Literary--Artistic--Political--
        Scientific"). Concludes that state and local courts
        will be able to determine SWAP and POW, but that the
        Supreme Court will remain the final arbiter of SLAPS.

288.   Wills, Garry. "Measuring the Impact of Erotica."
           Psychology Today, August 1977, pp. 30-34, 74-76.

        A critical analysis of the methods and findings of the
        Commission on Obscenity and Pornography. Challenges
        research designs in surveys, and in quasi- and controlled
        experiments, and criticizes nature of the samples and
        inconsistencies in findings. Centers on the Commission's
        inability to study the effects of erotica on children.

289.   Wohl, Burton. "The Reluctant Pornographer." *Harper's
           Magazine*, December 1976, pp. 91-94.

        Literary reminiscences of the author's experience in
        a porno factory in Los Angeles. Describes the rise of
        the owner, "Uncle Mortie," the working conditions, and
        the way in which the author dealt with being in charge
        of the production of a pornographic book. Expresses
        the feelings of embarrassment and reluctance which he
        contends many struggling authors must feel working in
        the erotica business.

VI

GOVERNMENT DOCUMENTS

290. Abelson, H.; R. Cohen; E. Heaton; and C. Suder. "Public Attitudes Towards and Experience with Erotic Materials: Findings." *Technical Report of the Commission on Obscenity and Pornography: National Survey, vol. VI.* Washington, D.C.: U.S. Government Printing Office, 1971, pp. 1-137.

The findings of a national survey of adults and youths regarding erotica. Results reveal: (1) a substantial majority have been exposed to erotic materials; (2) few feel erotica is a serious problem; (3) most approve availability of materials for adults, though control is preferred in regard to TV and young people. Findings also indicate that those most likely to restrict availability lack exposure to erotica and favor limiting criticism of God, government and police.

291. Alschuler, Martha. "Origins of the Law of Obscenity." *Technical Report of the Commission on Obscenity and Pornography: Legal Analysis, vol. II.* Washington, D.C.: U.S. Government Printing Office, 1971, pp. 65-81.

A historical exegesis on the development of obscenity laws in England and the United States up to 1870. Author notes that early antiobscenity law was often associated with religious impiety and the prosecution of other morals offenses. Further, a correlation is drawn between controls on expression in literature and the increasing literacy of the lower classes.

292. Amoroso, Donald M.; Marvin Brown; Manfred Pruesse; Edward E. Ware; and Dennis W. Pilkey. "An Investigation of Behavioral, Psychological, and Physiological Reactions to Pornographic Stimuli." *Technical Report*

*of the Commission on Obscenity and Pornography: Erotica
and Social Behavior, vol. VIII.* Washington, D.C.:
U.S. Government Printing Office, 1971, pp. 1-40.

Investigation consisted of two studies: (1) 60 males
were shown slides involving erotica and asked to rate
them on pornographic content and pleasantness; and (2)
56 males were studied for time spent looking at slides
of erotica, both alone and with an audience. Findings
suggest that looking time decreased with presence of
audience, and that few items were rated as "hard-core."
Pornography tended to be seen as both stimulating and unpleasant when labeled as such. Little change in behavior
after exposure was reported.

293. Bender Paul. "Definition of 'Obscene' Under Existing
      Law." *Technical Report of the Commission on Obscenity
      and Pornography: Legal Analysis, vol. II.* Washington,
      D.C.: U.S. Government Printing Office, 1971, pp. 5-27.

      Discusses the various disputes over the meaning of
      "obscene" in general and specific statutes. Major cases
      and decisions, including *Regina* v. *Hicklin* and the Roth
      decision, are used to identify the present state of the
      definition. Author concludes that under general statute,
      absence of redeeming social value must be clear; while
      under specific statute, few guidelines have been devel-
      oped.

294. Bender, Paul. "Implications of *Stanley* v. *Georgia*."
      *Technical Report of the Commission on Obscenity and
      Pornography: Legal Analysis, vol. II.* Washington,
      D.C.: U.S. Government Printing Office, 1971, pp. 28-
      36.

      An analysis of the consequences of *Stanley* v. *Georgia*,
      particularly in regard to the court's equation of enter-
      tainment value with ideological value. The author notes
      that this makes the notion of "utter lack of redeeming
      social value" almost impossible to demonstrate; hence,
      prohibitions of pornography must be very narrowly based.

295. Ben-Veniste, Richard. "Pornography and Sex Crime: The
      Danish Experience." *Technical Report of the Commission
      on Obscenity and Pornography: Erotica and Antisocial
      Behavior, vol. VII.* Washington, D.C.: U.S. Government
      Printing Office, 1971, pp. 245-261.

      A study of the effects of sex-crime rate in Copenhagen
      and its implications for the hypothesis that availability

of erotica causes sex crimes. Examination of police
records indicates sharp decline in sex offenses. Author
speculates that this is due to increased sexual permissiveness and easy access to erotica. Link between sex
crimes and erotica is strongly denied.

296. Berger, Alan S.; John H. Gagnon; and William Simon.
"Pornography: High School and College Years." *Technical Report of the Commission on Obscenity and Pornography: The Consumer and the Community, vol. IX.*
Washington, D.C.: U.S. Government Printing Office,
1971, pp. 165-208.

1177 male and female undergraduates were interviewed
regarding their exposure to pornography and the findings
correlated with other aspects of their background and
development. Findings include: (1) pornographic exposure
does not occur in isolation but as a normal part of
adolescent experience; (2) individuals with high exposure
were more sexually active; (3) education is not a function
of erotica in the population; and (4) exposure occurs
often before college and continues throughout college
years.

297. Berger, Alan S.; John H. Gagnon; and William Simon.
"Urban Working Class Adolescents and Sexually Explicit
Media." *Technical Report of the Commission on Ob-
scenity and Pornography: The Consumer and the Community,
vol. IX.* Washington, D.C.: U.S. Government Printing
Office, 1971, pp. 209-271.

473 young people in Chicago responded to questionnaires
on the rates and sources of exposure to erotica. Results
included: (1) girls were less likely to be exposed; (2)
exposure frequently occurred through friends; (3) subjects generally felt their attitudes were more liberal
than those of their parents; (4) degree of social par-
ticipation correlated with exposure; and (5) exposure
is not strongly related to sexual activity or changes
in attitudes.

298. Brock, Timothy C. "Erotic Materials: A Commodity Theory
Analysis of Availability and Desirability." *Technical
Report of the Commission on Obscenity and Pornography:
Preliminary Studies, vol. I.* Washington, D.C.: U.S.
Government Printing Office, 1971, pp. 131-137.

Argues for the applicability of commodity-theory analysis when exploring the hypothesis that unavailability

of pornography increases its desirability. Brief discussion of the general features of the theory is coupled
with specific evidence for the theory. Implications for
erotic materials are explored.

299. Bromberger, Bryan. "Australia." *Technical Report of*
        the Commission on Obscenity and Pornography: Legal
        Analysis, vol. II. Washington, D.C.: U.S. Government
        Printing Office, 1971, pp. 109-123.

        A review of the present legal state of censorship of
        obscene literature in Australia. Tabular presentation
        of criminal sanctions for violators of antiobscenity
        legislation is provided.

300. Bromberger, Bryan. "United Kingdom." *Technical Report*
        of the Commission on Obscenity and Pornography: Legal
        Analysis, vol. II. Washington, D.C.: U.S. Government
        Printing Office, 1971, pp. 206-221.

        A discussion of the important acts pertaining to control
        of obscene materials in Britain. Included is the Obscene
        Publications Act of 1959, the Children and Young Persons
        Act of 1955 and the Theatres Act of 1968.

301. Byrne, Donn, and John Lamberth. "The Effect of Erotic
        Stimuli on Sex Arousal, Evaluative Responses, and Sub-
        sequent Behavior." *Technical Report of the Commission*
        on Obscenity and Pornography: Erotica and Social Be-
        havior, vol. VIII. Washington, D.C.: U.S. Government
        Printing Office, 1971, pp. 41-67.

        42 couples were exposed to photographic and literary
        erotica and tested before and after with a feelings
        scale. They were further asked to complete a question-
        naire regarding sexual activity one week following ex-
        posure. Findings included: (1) females were as aroused
        by erotica as males; (2) reactions to masturbation were
        a significant indicator of responses to other sexual
        material; and (3) effect of erotica on later sexual be-
        havior was negligible.

302. Commission on Obscenity and Pornography. *Report of the*
        Commission on Obscenity and Pornography. Washington,
        D.C.: U.S. Government Printing Office, 1970. 646pp.

        An overview of the activities of the Commission and a
        statement of findings and recommendations based in part
        on the Technical Report of the Commission. Includes:
        (1) a general review of the results suggested by the

Technical Report; (2) recommendations both nonlegislative
and legislative to federal, state and local governments; ·
(3) separate statements by Commission members; (4) reports from various Commission panels; and (5) appendices
including appropriate Public Laws creating the Commission,
and biographical data on members.

303.   Cook, Robert [sic for Royer] F., and Robert H. Fosen.
       "Pornography and the Sex Offender: Patterns of Exposure
       and Immediate Arousal of Effects of Pornographic Stim-
       uli." *Technical Report of the Commission on Obscenity
       and Pornography: Erotica and Antisocial Behavior, vol.
       VIII*. Washington, D.C.: U.S. Government Printing
       Office, 1971, pp. 149-162.

       A study of sex offenders and criminal-code violators
       in Wisconsin State Prison. Subjects viewed slides of
       various sexual behaviors and were subsequently interviewed
       regarding past contact with erotica. Findings indicate
       no significant differences were found regarding arousal
       responses; however, sex offenders were found to have less
       past exposure to pornographic materials.

304.   Damaska, Mirjan. "France." *Technical Report of the
       Commission on Obscenity and Pornography: Legal Analysis,
       vol. II*. Washington, D.C.: U.S. Government Printing
       Office, 1971, pp. 148-159.

       A general account of the laws pertaining to obscene
       materials in France. Areas discussed include the French
       Penal Code, publications oriented toward juveniles,
       administrative controls over publication, motion pictures,
       radio, television and theatrical performances.

305.   Damaska, Mirjan. "Hungary and the Soviet Union." *Tech-
       nical Report of the Commission on Obscenity and Pornog-
       raphy: Legal Analysis, vol. II*. Washington, D.C.:
       U.S. Government Printing Office, 1971, pp. 160-164.

       To alleviate Westerners' ignorance about antiobscenity
       legislation in Hungary and the U.S.S.R., the author
       provides an abbreviated account of the laws relating to
       erotic expression. Author notes that a lack of materials
       which Westerners would call "obscene" is a consequence
       of prohibitive and restrictive standards in these coun-
       tries.

306.   Damaska, Mirjan. "Italy." *Technical Report of the
       Commission on Obscenity and Pornography: Legal Analysis,*

vol. II. Washington, D.C.: U.S. Government Printing
Office, 1971, pp. 175-185.

A review of the relevant statutes relating to obscenity
and pornography in Italy. Obscenity is statutorily defined and relates to acts and objects "offensive to
shame." A discussion of laws relating to trafficking
of erotic materials, media censorship and press law is
included.

307. Damaska, Mirjan. "West Germany." *Technical Report of
the Commission on Obscenity and Pornography: Legal
Analysis, vol. II.* Washington, D.C.: U.S. Government
Printing Office, 1971, pp. 222-232.

An overview of the statutes relating to the regulation
of obscene materials in West Germany. Author notes that
the concept of obscenity or pornography is subsumed under
the concept of "lewdness" in German law. Control of
erotica for juveniles and erotic expression in the mass
media are specifically discussed.

308. Damaska, Mirjan. "Yugoslavia." *Technical Report of the
Commission on Obscenity and Pornography: Legal Analysis,
vol. II.* Washington, D.C.: U.S. Government Printing
Office, 1971, pp. 233-241.

A discussion of laws relating to the control of erotic
materials in Yugoslavia. Author notes that there is
considerable liberality regarding such materials there,
in contrast to other European countries. Eastern obscenity is broadly defined as expressions "seriously
injurious to morality," a phrase accommodating much in
its ambiguity.

309. Davis, Keith E., and George N. Braucht. "Exposure to
Pornography, Character, and Sexual Deviance: A Retro-
spective Survey." *Technical Report of the Commission
on Obscenity and Pornography: Erotica and Antisocial
Behavior, vol. VII.* Washington, D.C.: U.S. Government
Printing Office, 1971, pp. 173-248.

Employing a retrospective, cross-sectional design, the
authors examine the postulated link between exposure to
erotica, moral character and deviant sexual behavior.
Prison inmates, Mexican-Americans, Blacks, college students and seminary students were among the 375 males
used for the sample. Findings suggested a modest relationship between exposure and low moral character,
but only for those exposed after the age of 17.

310. Davis, Keith E., and George N. Braucht. "Reactions to Viewing Films of Erotically Realistic Heterosexual Behavior." *Technical Report of the Commission on Obscenity and Pornography: Erotica and Social Behavior, vol. VIII.* Washington, D.C.: U.S. Government Printing Office, 1971, pp. 58-96.

    A pre- and post-test design was employed to explore sexual responses and behavior of subjects following exposure to erotica. Subjects experienced increased arousal, with those most highly aroused having limited heterosexual experience or some homosexual experience. Increased heterosexual activity was noted for the 24 hours subsequent to exposure.

311. Elias, James. "Exposure of Adolescents to Erotic Materials." *Technical Report of the Commission on Obscenity and Pornography: The Consumer and the Community, vol. IX.* Washington, D.C.: U.S. Government Printing Office, 1971, pp. 273-311.

    High school students in an urban area responded to questionnaires and interviews regarding exposure to and purpose of erotica. Males were found to have a greater degree of exposure, and religious participation correlated negatively with exposure. No generalizations could be made on respondents' attitudes toward pornographic materials, since opinions differed widely.

312. Finkelstein, M. Marvin. "The Traffic in Sex-Oriented Materials in Boston." *Technical Report of the Commission on Obscenity and Pornography: The Marketplace: Empirical Studies, vol. IV.* Washington, D.C.: U.S. Government Printing Office, 1971, pp. 99-154.

    A study of adult bookstores in Boston including those located in the "Combat Zone." Methods included interviews with patrons, law enforcement officers, researchers and members of the press. Criminal records were checked and bookstores inspected. Areas explored included employees, materials available, distribution and production of materials, and arrests for violations of obscenity laws.

313. Finkelstein, M. Marvin. "Traffic in Sex-Oriented Materials and Criminality and Organized Crime: The Relationship." *Technical Report of the Commission on Obscenity and Pornography: Societal Control Mechanisms, vol. V.* Washington, D.C.: U.S. Government Printing Office, 1971, pp. 61-79.

Authors conducted a study in Boston regarding the
criminal records of 63 operators and employees of stores
selling pornographic materials. Results suggested a
definite pattern of criminal activity, with those enter-
ing the business after 1966 being particularly active
criminally. A second study was conducted on organized-
crime connections in New York, Los Angeles, Chicago,
Boston and San Francisco. Strong suspicions of a link
were asserted in New York, but the evidence for other
cities was inconclusive.

314. Friedman, Jane. "Regulation of Obscenity by Federal
      Agencies." *Technical Report of the Commission on Ob-
      scenity and Pornography: Societal Control Mechanisms,
      vol. V.* Washington, D.C.: U.S. Government Printing
      Office, 1971, pp. 15-34.

      A discussion of the regulatory function of the Post
      Office and Customs Bureau regarding the control of erot-
      ica. The specific ways and means for control were ex-
      plored along with court decisions and historical per-
      spectives which guide the activities of the federal
      agencies.

315. Friedman, Jane M. "State Obscenity Statutes: Descrip-
      tion and Analysis." *Technical Report of the Commis-
      sion on Obscenity and Pornography: Legal Analysis,
      vol. II.* Washington, D.C.: U.S. Government Printing
      Office, 1971, pp. 37-61.

      A general review of pornography and obscenity laws in
      the 50 states and the District of Columbia. Statutory
      definitions, penalties, immunities, minors statutes and
      civil enforcement procedures are among the areas dis-
      cussed.

316. Glide Foundation. "Effects of Erotic Stimuli Used in
      National Sex Forum Training Courses in Human Sexual-
      ity." *Technical Report of the Commission on Obscenity
      and Pornography: Societal Control Mechanisms, vol. V.*
      Washington, D.C.: U.S. Government Printing Office,
      1971, pp. 354-368.

      A study of participants' training experiences and
      reactions to exposure to erotic materials as part of the
      National Sex Forum Training Courses. Data obtained pri-
      marily from questionnaires indicated that respondents
      were well-adjusted, and reacted to materials with curi-
      osity and interest, and with some arousal. Few indicated
      interest in engaging in new types of sex after exposure.

317. Goldstein, Michael J.; Harold S. Kant; Lewis L. Judd;
      Clinton J. Rice; and Richard Green. "Exposure to
      Pornography and Sexual Behavior in Deviant and Normal
      Groups." *Technical Report of the Commission on Ob-
      scenity and Pornography: Erotica and Antisocial Be-
      havior, vol. VII*. Washington, D.C.: U.S. Government
      Printing Office, 1971, pp. 1-89.

      Sample in study included sex deviates, users of por-
      nography, Blacks and Caucasians. Results indicated that
      sex deviates had less access to pornography as adoles-
      cents than controls, and that sex attitudes and behaviors
      are more strongly affected by family and cultural environ-
      ment. Further, no specific type of sexual behavior is
      associated with exposure; behavior depends more on in-
      ternal attitudes and availability of a partner. Ques-
      tionnaires and tabular data are included.

318. Hocker, Peter. "Japan." *Technical Report of the Com-
      mission on Obscenity and Pornography: Legal Analysis,
      vol. II*. Washington, D.C.: U.S. Government Printing
      Office, 1971, pp. 186-189.

      A look at the main statutory provisions governing
      Japan's obscenity laws. Obscenity arises if an object
      or material injures a man's sense of shame, stimulates
      the sexual desires or is contrary to the prevailing
      sexual morality.

319. Holland, Norman N. "Pornography and the Mechanisms of
      Defense." *Technical Report of the Commission on Ob-
      scenity and Pornography: Preliminary Studies, vol. I*.
      Washington, D.C.: U.S. Government Printing Office,
      1971, pp. 115-129.

      Pornography is treated as a special type of literature
      and a fantasy-defense model is advanced in order to
      study the adaptive aspects of subjects. Author asserts
      that affective responses to pornography depend as much
      on what the subject brings to the text as on what the
      text brings to the subject. No scientific evidence is
      available to support the notion that pornography makes
      permanent changes in character, and author argues against
      interference in the freedom to read such materials.

320. Howard, James L.; Clifford B. Reifler; and Myron B.
      Liptzin. "Effects of Exposure to Pornography."
      *Technical Report of the Commission on Obscenity and
      Pornography: Erotica and Social Behavior, vol. VIII*.

Washington, D.C.: U.S. Government Printing Office, 1971, pp. 97-132.

Authors coupled the psychological measures of self-report, standardized tests and psychiatric interviews with physiological measures (penile erection, acid phosphatase secretion and heart rate), to measure the effects on 23 subjects to exposure to erotica, 90 minutes a day for 15 days. Findings indicate erotica is a harmless stimulus with no permanent attitudinal or behavioral effects.

321. Johnson, Weldon T.; Lenore R. Kupperstein; and Joseph J. Peters. "Sex Offenders' Experience with Erotica." *Technical Report of the Commission on Obscenity and Pornography: Erotica and Antisocial Behavior, vol. VII.* Washington, D.C.: U.S. Government Printing Office, 1971, pp. 163-171.

47 white males convicted of sex crimes were examined in regard to past exposure to pornography, and results compared with findings in a recent national probability survey (Abelson et al. 1971). Results indicated that no significant difference could be found in relation to past exposure to erotica. Authors contend experience with pornography cannot be considered a differentiating factor between deviants and controls.

322. Kant, Harold S.; Michael J. Goldstein; and Derek J. Lepper. "A Pilot Comparison of Two Research Instruments Measuring Exposure to Pornography." *Technical Report of the Commission on Obscenity and Pornography: Erotica and Antisocial Behavior, vol. VII.* Washington, D.C.: U.S. Government Printing Office, 1971, pp. 325-340.

Two test instruments (Temple and LBI) were compared for function and effectiveness in regard to testing attitudes and behaviors related to exposure to erotica. LBI and Temple data were similar, LBI more successfully revealing the number of exposures.

323. Katzman, Marshall. "Photograph Characteristics Influencing the Judgment of Obscenity." *Technical Report of the Commission on Obscenity and Pornography: The Consumer and the Community, vol. IX.* Washington, D.C.: U.S. Government Printing Office, 1971, pp. 9-26.

Based on a previous study of 314 subjects rating photographs as to obscenity, the author assigned values to 46

specific characteristics of the photographs, and correlated those values with obscenity scores. Findings
suggested: (1) most characteristics correlated with
obscenity judgments; (2) subgroups tended to agree on
which characteristics correlated highly with obscenity
judgments; and (3) correlations of nudity with obscenity
were higher for lower socioeconomic groups.

324. Katzman, Marshall. "Relationship of Socioeconomic Back-
    ground to Judgments of Sexual Stimulation: Correlation
    with Judgments of Obscenity." *Technical Report of the
    Commission on Obscenity and Pornography: The Consumer
    and the Community, vol. IX.* Washington, D.C.: U.S.
    Government Printing Office, 1971, pp. 1-7.

    Based on an earlier study in which 285 men were shown
    90 erotic photographs and asked to rate them in regard
    to obscenity and stimulation. Author correlates ob-
    scenity judgments and sexual stimulation with educational
    and occupational data. Conclusions suggest: (1) a low posi-
    tive correlation between stimulation and obscenity judg-
    ments; (2) nudity is a greater stimulus factor for lower
    educational groups; (3) the higher the educational level,
    the lower the correlation between obscenity and stimulus
    judgments.

325. Kupperstein, Lenore. "The Role of Pornography in the
    Etiology of Juvenile Delinquency: A Review of the
    Literature." *Technical Report of the Commission on
    Obscenity and Pornography: Preliminary Studies, vol.
    I.* Washington, D.C.: U.S. Government Printing Office,
    1971, pp. 103-111.

    A review of 39 books and articles (12 cited) on delin-
    quency, focusing particularly on the relationship between
    pornography and obscenity and juvenile delinquency. Con-
    cludes there is no significant evidence of causal links
    between erotic literature and delinquent acts.

326. Kupperstein, Lenore R., and W. Cody Wilson. "Erotica
    and Antisocial Behavior: An Analysis of Selected Social
    Indicator Statistics." *Technical Report of the Com-
    mission on Obscenity and Pornography: Erotica and Anti-
    social Behavior, vol. VII.* Washington, D.C.: U.S.
    Government Printing Office, 1971, pp. 311-323.

    A general analysis of crime data in the 1960s to ex-
    plore the possibility of a causal link between increased
    availability of erotica and sex crimes. The social in-

dices included: (1) circulation of *Playboy* magazine; (2)
rate of sex crimes; (3) national police statistics on
crime in general; (4) adult and juvenile crime data; and
(5) illegitimacy rates. Analysis indicated no relation
between access to erotica, and crime or illegitimacy
rates.

327. Kutschinsky, Berl. "The Effect of Pornography: A Pilot
      Experiment on Perception, Behavior, and Attitudes."
      *Technical Report of the Commission on Obscenity and
      Pornography: Erotica and Social Behavior, vol. VIII.*
      Washington, D.C.: U.S. Government Printing Office,
      1971, pp. 133-169.

      72 students, mostly Danish married couples, were sub-
      jected to pornographic films, readings and photography,
      for one hour. Pre- and post-tests were employed to as-
      sess changes in behavior and attitudes. Findings re-
      vealed: (1) strong emotional reactions to pornography
      were rare; (2) no increase in deviant sexual practices
      was observed; and (3) viewers expressed little interest
      in seeing more pornography after one-hour exposure.

328. Kutschinsky, Berl. "Pornography in Denmark: Pieces of
      a Jigsaw Puzzle Collected Around New Year 1970."
      *Technical Report of the Commission on Obscenity and
      Pornography: The Marketplace: Empirical Studies, vol.
      IV.* Washington, D.C.: U.S. Government Printing Office,
      1971, pp. 263-288.

      A general exploration into the uses and marketing of
      pornography in Copenhagen. Customers were observed at
      shops distributing pornographic materials; age, time
      spent and purchases were noted. A study was also con-
      ducted on public attitudes toward erotica. General
      acceptance was noted, though a significant minority felt
      it was harmful.

329. Kutschinsky, Berl. "Towards an Explanation of the De-
      crease in Registered Sex Crimes in Copenhagen."
      *Technical Report of the Commission on Obscenity and
      Pornography: Erotica and Antisocial Behavior, vol. VII.*
      Washington, D.C.: U.S. Government Printing Office,
      1971, pp. 263-310.

      A representative sample of 400 persons in Copenhagen
      were subjects of an interview-investigation in an attempt
      to explain the sharp decrease of reported sex crimes in
      the city following widespread access to erotica. Subjects

were queried regarding their experience as victims of
sex crimes, the definition of a sex crime, their attitudes toward reporting such crimes and toward the crimes
themselves. A significant but tentative conclusion is
drawn that availability of erotica may have directly
caused a decrease in peeping and physical indecency
toward girls.

330. Livneh, Ernst. "Israel." *Technical Report of the Commission on Obscenity and Pornography: Legal Analysis,
vol. II.* Washington, D.C.: U.S. Government Printing
Office, 1971, pp. 165-174.

A review of the laws and regulations pertaining to
pornography and obscenity in Israel. Author indicates
foundation of Israeli law was built upon the British
Mandatory Government of Palestine, and little law has
developed to resolve many open issues.

331. LoSciuto, L.; A. Spector; E. Michels; and C. Jenne.
"Public Attitudes Towards and Experience with Erotic
Materials: Methodological Report." *Technical Report
of the Commission on Obscenity and Pornography: National
Survey, vol. VI.* Washington, D.C.: U.S. Government
Printing Office, 1971, pp. 139-256.

A discussion and presentation of the methodology of
the National Survey of adults and adolescents regarding
experience with and attitudes toward erotica. Areas
of analysis include: (1) sample and study design; (2)
questionnaires; (3) interviewer selection and training;
(4) completion rates; (5) field procedure; and (6) coding
and editing practices. Forms and questionnaires employed
are included.

332. Mann, Jay; Jack Sidman; and Sheldon Starr. "Effects of
Erotic Films on Sexual Behavior of Married Couples."
*Technical Report of the Commission on Obscenity and
Pornography: Erotica and Social Behavior, vol. VIII.*
Washington, D.C.: U.S. Government Printing Office,
1971, pp. 170-254.

85 married couples were placed in groups; some were
exposed to erotic films, some to nonerotic films. No significant changes in regard to behavior or attitude were
found in comparing the groups subsequent to exposure,
except that couples viewing erotica increased their
sexual activity on film-viewing nights.

333. Massey, Morris E. "A Marketing Analysis of Sex-Oriented
      Materials: A Pilot Study in Denver, August 1969."
      Technical Report of the Commission on Obscenity and
      Pornography: The Marketplace: Empirical Studies, vol.
      IV. Washington, D.C.: U.S. Government Printing Office,
      1971, pp. 3-98.

      Using observation and interview techniques, the author
      studied marketing activities, environment and community
      climate in relation to the distribution of sex-oriented
      materials in Denver. Many conclusions were drawn, in-
      cluding: (1) erotic materials are best seen as substi-
      tutes for real sexual satisfaction; (2) retail outlets
      were usually located downtown and run as small businesses;
      (3) 60% of local inventories were supplied by one whole-
      saler; and (4) community had differing notions as to
      what is pornographic.

334. Money, John. "The Positive and Constructive Approach
      to Pornography: In General Sex Education, in the Home,
      and in Sexological Counseling." *Technical Report of*
      the Commission on Obscenity and Pornography: Societal
      Control Mechanisms, vol. V. Washington, D.C.: U.S.
      Government Printing Office, 1971, pp. 339-353.

      An examination of the positive uses of erotica for
      children and adults. Erotic materials have traditionally
      been forbidden, and consequently children have used the
      material as a form of defiance. The author contends
      that erotica should become part of the home and a topic
      of rational discussion. Further, the material could be
      used as a form of sex education for adults and children.

335. Mosher, Donald L. "Psychological Reactions to Porno-
      graphic Films." *Technical Report of the Commission*
      on Obscenity and Pornography: Erotica and Social Be-
      havior, vol. VIII. Washington, D.C.: U.S. Government
      Printing Office, 1971, pp. 255-312.

      377 male and female undergraduates were shown two por-
      nographic films and their responses studied. Males were
      found to be more aroused and activated by oral-genital
      relations, while women with high sex guilt viewed such
      acts negatively. Subjects had more conversations and
      sex fantasies in the 24 hours subsequent to exposure,
      and experienced a decrease in sex callousness toward
      women.

336. Mosher, Donald L., and Harvey Katz. "Pornographic Films,
      Male Verbal Aggression Against Women and Guilt."
      *Technical Report of the Commission on Obscenity and
      Pornography: Erotica and Social Behavior, vol. VIII.*
      Washington, D.C.: U.S. Government Printing Office,
      1971, pp. 357-379.

      A study of the influence of erotic materials on verbal
      aggression against women. 125 men were exposed to erotic
      and nonerotic films. Subjects were then told they could
      view another film which would be pornographic depending
      on their aggressiveness toward a female assistant. Find-
      ings suggest that sexual arousal from erotica does not
      increase aggressiveness toward women.

337. Nawy, Harold. "The San Francisco Erotic Marketplace."
      *Technical Report of the Commission on Obscenity and
      Pornography: The Marketplace: Empirical Studies, vol.
      IV.* Washington, D.C.: U.S. Government Printing
      Office, 1971, pp. 155-224.

      Two general purposes are stated for this study: (1)
      "to determine the extent and nature of the distribution
      of sex-oriented material in San Francisco" and (2) "to
      describe and analyze the sociological and psychological
      attitudes, experiences and behaviors of the consumer popu-
      lation." In part, the study concluded: (1) no evidence of
      organized crime could be found; (2) general community
      standards did not find the materials obscene; and (3) the
      majority of consumers are middle-class, middle-aged white
      males.

338. Propper, Martin M. "Exposure to Sexually Oriented Mate-
      rials Among Young Male Prisoners." *Technical Report
      of the Commission on Obscenity and Pornography: The
      Consumer and the Community, vol. IX.* Washington, D.C.:
      U.S. Government Printing Office, 1971, pp. 313-404.

      464 incarcerated males ranging in age from 16 to 21
      were studied regarding exposure to erotica, and atti-
      tudinal and behavioral relationships. Findings suggested
      that inmates were exposed visually between the ages of
      6 and 11, with textual exposure at 15 or 16. High ex-
      posure correlated with greater variety of sexual prac-
      tices.

339. Randall, Richard S. "Classification by the Motion Pic-
      ture Industry." *Technical Report of the Commission on
      Obscenity and Pornography: Societal Control Mechanisms,
      vol. V.* Washington, D.C.: U.S. Government Printing
      Office, 1971, pp. 219-292.

An exposition of the rating system established by the
Motion Picture Association of America for films. Historical and analytical approaches are employed and the mechanisms of the rating system itself are presented.

340. Roach, William J., and Louise Kreisberg. "Westchester
      College Students' Views on Pornography." *Technical
      Report of the Commission on Obscenity and Pornography:
      Preliminary Studies, vol. I.* Washington, D.C.: U.S.
      Government Printing Office, 1971, pp. 185-189.

      Consists primarily of tabular data obtained from 625
      students from eight colleges in Westchester County, New
      York. Results indicated that pornography is ill-defined,
      that exposure frequently occurred at an early age, and
      that little effect on personal behavior or attitudes is
      acknowledged.

341. Sampson, John J. "Commercial Traffic in Sexually Oriented
      Materials." *Technical Report of the Commission on
      Obscenity and Pornography, vol. III.* Washington, D.C.:
      U.S. Government Printing Office, 1971, pp. 1-208.

      Examines the commercial aspects of pornography, in-
      cluding the means by which these materials are distributed,
      exhibited and sold. Conclusions of the study include:
      (1) various forms of pornography are widespread; (2)
      the market for such materials is very large; and (3) ex-
      plicit materials are much the same as those distributed
      in Denmark. No predictions on the direction of the mar-
      ket are made, though there is some belief that the degree
      of explicitness in these materials will not change sig-
      nificantly in the coming years.

342. Schiller, Patricia. "Effects of Mass Media on the Sexual
      Behavior of Adolescent Females." *Technical Report of
      the Commission on Obscenity and Pornography: Prelimi-
      nary Studies, vol. I.* Washington, D.C.: U.S. Govern-
      ment Printing Office, 1971, pp. 191-195.

      Data on the influence of pornographic materials on
      female sexual behavior was obtained from girls in a two-
      year community college and from the Webster School for
      pregnant girls. Author observed that the girls were
      rarely exposed to hard-core pornography, but read works
      closely associating love and sex. Romantic content in
      media seemed to have significant behavioral effect.

343. Silving, Helen. "Argentina." *Technical Report of the Commission on Obscenity and Pornography: Legal Analysis, vol. II.* Washington, D.C.: U.S. Government Printing Office, 1971, pp. 93-108.

Provides a general account of the laws and court cases relating to obscenity, including films and theater performances, in Argentina. Historical developments affecting interpretation of the laws are discussed, and specific passages in the constitution and legal code are cited.

344. Silving, Helen. "Mexico." *Technical Report of the Commission on Obscenity and Pornography: Legal Analysis, vol. II.* Washington, D.C.: U.S. Government Printing Office, 1971, pp. 190-205.

Constitutional acts and statutory laws relating to obscenity and pornography are identified and discussed. Judicial interpretations with specific case citations are provided.

345. Smith, Alexander B., and Bernard Locke. "Problems in Arrests and Prosecutions for Obscenity and Pornography: Responses of Police and Prosecutors." *Technical Report of the Commission on Obscenity and Pornography: Societal Control Mechanisms, vol. V.* Washington, D.C.: U.S. Government Printing Office, 1971, pp. 35-60.

Police and prosecutors in 17 major cities were interviewed. City sizes ranged from 350,000 to the three largest cities in the U.S. Most police felt that enforcement is of low priority, and that there is little community involvement in the problem. Police and prosecutors expressed frustration over inability to get convictions, and suspected relationships with organized crime.

346. Sonenschein, David; Mark J.M. Ross; Richard Bauman; Linda Swartz; and Morgan MacLachlan. "A Study of Mass Media Erotica: A Romance or Confession Magazine." *Technical Report of the Commission on Obscenity and Pornography: The Consumer and the Community, vol. IX.* Washington, D.C.: U.S. Government Printing Office, 1971, pp. 99-164.

An anthropological analysis of the significance of confession magazines in our culture. The magazines, stories, publishers and readers are studied with specific attention to sexual themes and their effects on readers. Notes that narrator is usually young female, and that sexual activity is relatively slight, with emphasis on emotions and guilt. Readers tended to be young, read for entertainment and did not consider the material pornographic. Publishers indicated desire to emotionally arouse the reader.

347. Tannenbaum, Percy H. "Emotional Arousal as a Mediator of Erotic Communication Effects." *Technical Report of the Commission on Obscenity and Pornography: Erotica and Social Behavior, vol. VIII.* Washington, D.C.: U.S. Government Printing Office, 1971, pp. 326-356.

The author employs an emotional arousal model to analyze behavior of subjects subsequent to exposure to erotica. Findings indicate higher level of aggressive behavior related to arousal from erotica than from aggressiveness portrayed in films with less arousal potential.

348. Thornberry, Terrence P., and Robert A. Silverman. "Exposure to Pornography and Juvenile Delinquency: The Relationship as Indicated by Juvenile Court Records." *Technical Report of the Commission on Obscenity and Pornography: Preliminary Studies, vol. I.* Washington, D.C.: U.S. Government Printing Office, 1971, pp. 175-179.

Court case records of 436 juveniles were examined to study the generally held contention that pornography causes juvenile sex crimes. In not one instance did the records indicate that pornography played a role in the criminal acts.

349. U.S. Congress, House, Committee on Post Office and Civil Service, *Anti-Obscenity Legislation: Hearings on H.R. 2159*, 92nd Congress, 1st Session, 28 April 1971 and 5 May 1971. 108pp.

Hearings on a bill to exclude mail which offers minors materials that are considered obscene. Individuals testifying are Thomas Asher, Dr. Armand Di Francesco, the Hon. Thaddeus J. Dulski, Rev. Morton A. Hill and the Hon. David A. Nelson. Statements submitted by Thomas R. Asher, the Hon. Edward J. Derwinski, Robert W. Frase, Robert H. Mollohan and the Hon. Chalmers P. Wylie. Includes text of bill.

350. U.S. Congress, House, Committee on Post Office and Civil
Service, *Obscenity in the Mails: Hearings*, 91st Congress, 2nd Session, 11 August 1970-18 November 1970.
185pp.

Hearings on the President's Commission on Obscenity
and Pornography and a bill (HR 19541) to define obscene
mail for the purpose of protecting individual rights to
privacy. Testimony and statements were taken from
Congressmen and the following individuals: Bernard L.
Bonniwell, Dr. Victor B. Cline, Dr. Albert Hobbs, Dr.
James L. Howard, William E. Schluter, Natalie Shainers,
Charles W. Socarides, Lawrence Speiser, Dr. Sheldon
Starr, Melvin Anchell, John R. Cavanaugh, Irwin Karp,
the Hon. David A. Nelson, and Weil, Gostshal and Manges,
Counsel, Association of American Publishers, Inc. Also
includes pertinent articles reprinted from various
periodicals.

351. U.S. Congress, House, Committee on Post Office and Civil
Service, *Obscenity in the Mails: Hearings on H.R.
10867: Part I*, 91st Congress, 1st Session, 5-6 August
1969. 199pp.

Hearings on excluding mail offering obscene materials,
especially to minors. Testimony and statements are included from Congressmen and the following individuals:
the Hon. David Nelson, James Rademacher, Will Wilson
and members of the Commission on Obscenity and Pornography.
Includes text of bill and reprints of pertinent articles
from periodicals.

352. U.S. Congress, House, Committee on Post Office and Civil
Service, *Obscenity in the Mails: Hearings on H.R.
10867: Part II*, 91st Congress, 1st Session, 1 October
1969-10 December 1969. 510pp.

Hearings on excluding mail offering obscene materials,
especially to minors. Testimony and statements are included from Congressmen and the following individuals:
Earl Franklin, Raymond Gauer, the Hon. Theodore S. Kasler,
Mario A. Procaccino, Lawrence Speiser, Harry Thayer,
Jack Chernus, Irwin Karp, Horace S. Manges, William D.
Pfender, and the Hon. William H. Rehnquist. Also includes
additional communications and pertinent articles reprinted
from periodicals.

353. U.S. Congress, House, Committee on the Judiciary, *Anti-
obscenity Legislation: Hearings on H.R. 5171, H.R.*

11009, *H.R. 11031, H.R. 11032 and Related Measures*,
91st Congress, 1st Session, 25 September 1969–16 April
1970. 1222pp.

Hearings on pending obscenity legislation. Statements
are included from the following individuals: Harry M.
Clor, Ambrose Doskow, Sheldon H. Elsen, Raymond P. Gauer,
Charles D. Hawley, Rev. Morton A. Hill, Irwin Karp,
Richard Kuh, Rev. John McLaughlin, Horace S. Manges,
the Hon. William H. Rehnquist, Lawrence Speiser, Jack
Valenti and Dr. W. Cody Wilson. Also includes state-
ments from Congressmen and texts of pornography bills.

354.   U.S. Congress, House, Committee on the Judiciary, *Sexual
       Exploitation of Children: Hearings*, 95th Congress, 1st
       Session, 23 May 1977–20 September 1977. 477pp.

Hearings on prohibiting the sexual abuse of children
for the production and sale of pornographic materials.
Individuals testifying include the following: C. Neil
Benson, Judianne Densen-Gerber, G.R. Dickerson, Herald
Price Fahringer, Lenor M. Ferber, Heather Grant Florence,
Larry Flynt, Robert G. Gemignani, John C. Keeney, Robert
F. Leonard, Kenneth Maddy, Lloyd H. Martin, Bruce Nestande,
Donald Nicholson, Larry E. Parrish, Charles Rembar, Kurt
Simileo, Michael Sneed, the Hon. Richard R. Wier, Philip
Wilens and Kenneth Wooder. Also includes statements by
Barbara Scott, Robin M. Llcyd, Stephen P. Hutchinson,
Dr. Melvin Anchell, Marriane E. Cahill and selected
Congressmen. Reprints of pertinent articles also in-
cluded.

355.   U.S. Congress, Senate, Committee on Post Office and Civil
       Service, *Obscenity: Hearings on S 3220*, 91st Congress,
       2nd Session, 1 September 1970. 60pp.

Hearings on a bill to protect individual privacy by
allowing that material designated as obscene or offensive
mail can be returned at the mailer's expense. Statements
included from the following individuals: the Hon. Barry
M. Goldwater, the Hon. Mike Mansfield, the Hon. David A.
Nelson and Lawrence Speiser. Text of some amendments included.

356.   U.S. Congress, Senate, Committee on the Judiciary, *Juve-
       nile Delinquency: Hearings on S. Res. 342: Pornography
       and Obscenity: Part 22*, 91st Congress, 2nd Session,
       23 September 1970. 369pp.

Hearings on juvenile delinquency as it relates to the
potential detrimental effects pornographic material may
have on the behavior of young people. The following in-

dividuals testified: Dr. Victor B. Cline, Rev. Morton A.
Hill and Rev. Winfrey C. Link. Also includes exhibits
indicating pertinent research.

357. U.S. Congress, Senate, Committee on the Judiciary,
*Presidential Commission: Implementation of Recommenda-
tions of Presidential and National Commissions*, 92nd
Congress, 1st Session, 25 May 1971-27 July 1971.
360pp.

Includes an in-depth response by William B. Lockhardt
to the criticisms advanced against the Presidential
Commission on Obscenity and Pornography. Memoranda are
produced, and specific areas of concern are discussed
at length. General comments and recommendations regarding future commissions are made.

358. U.S. Congress, Senate, Committee on the Judiciary, *Protection of Children Against Sexual Exploitation: Hearings before the Subcommittee to Investigate Juvenile
Delinquency*, 95th Congress, 1st Session, 27 May 1977
and 16 June 1977. 158pp.

Provides statements given at hearings on legislation
for the control of sexual exploitation of children particularly as it relates to the use of children in pornographic materials. The views of lawyers, political
figures, producers and child participants are included
in the statements. Attention is paid to how children
are motivated to engage in pornographic activities and
to the best legislative methods to prevent the continu-
ance of such activities.

359. U.S. Congress, Senate, Committee on the Judiciary, *Protection of Children Against Sexual Exploitation Act
of 1977: Report on S 1585*, 95th Congress, 1st Session,
16 September 1977. 34pp.

Reports the findings of the Senate Committee. Committee
concluded: (1) child pornography is a highly organized
and wealthy industry; (2) using children as prostitutes
is harmful to children and society; (3) mails are significantly involved in the traffic of child pornography;
and (4) more federal laws are needed to prevent this
type of child abuse. Includes section-by-section analysis of S 1585.

360. Waaben, Knud. "Denmark, Sweden, and Norway." *Technical
Report of the Commission on Obscenity and Pornography:
Legal Analysis, vol. II*. Washington, D.C.: U.S.
Government Printing Office, 1971, pp. 127-147.

An overview of the laws and court practice relating
to pornographic materials in Denmark, Sweden and Norway.
A comparison is made between considerable liberality in
pornography laws in Denmark and comparative conservatism
in Norway.

361. Walker, C. Eugene. "Erotic Stimuli and the Aggressive
      Sexual Offender." *Technical Report of the Commission
      on Obscenity and Pornography: Erotica and Antisocial
      Behavior, vol. VII.* Washington, D.C.: U.S. Govern-
      ment Printing Office, 1971, pp. 91-147.

Purpose of the study was to determine if sex offenders
were exposed to pornography more frequently than nonsex
offenders, and if their thoughts and fantasies were
different when exposed. Subjects were interviewed, given
one objective and two projective tests. Results indicated that controls were exposed to pornography more
frequently and at a younger age than sex offenders.
Appendices include interview questions and tests.

362. Wallace, Douglas; Gerald Wehmer; and Edward Podany.
      "Contemporary Community Standards of Visual Erotica."
      *Technical Report of the Commission on Obscenity and
      Pornography: The Consumer and the Community, vol. IX.*
      Washington, D.C.: U.S. Government Printing Office,
      1971, pp. 27-87.

Subjects were exposed to slides of erotica, and response
booklets were provided. Findings suggest that there is
little agreement as to what is acceptable, though authors
found significant bimodal distributions. Church and
social service categories were labeled as "conservative-
intolerant," while students and professionals were considered "liberal-tolerant." Religiosity seemed to be
the most significant determiner of negative correlations.

363. White, David Manning, and Lewis D. Barnett. "College
      Students' Attitudes on Pornography: A Pilot Study."
      *Technical Report of the Commission on Obscenity and
      Pornography: Preliminary Studies, vol. I.* Washington,
      D.C.: U.S. Government Printing Office, 1971, pp. 181-
      189.

Consists primarily of tabular data obtained by a single
interviewer from 300 college students at five eastern
universities. Results indicated that they were first
exposed to pornography in childhood, usually from friends.
Little agreement could be found on a definition of pornography, and few felt any effects from exposure.

364. Wilson, W. Cody; Jane Friedman; and Bernard Horowitz.
     "Gravity of the Pornography Situation and Problems
     of Control." *Technical Report of the Commission on
     Obscenity and Pornography: Societal Control Mecha-
     nisms, vol. V.* Washington, D.C.: U.S. Government
     Printing Office, 1971, pp. 5-14.

     District and Municipal Attorneys were surveyed by
     questionnaire on their perceptions of the pornography
     problem and the difficulties of enforcement. In the
     larger cities, attorneys felt that the problem was more
     serious, that laws were more difficult to enforce and
     that there was a greater need to clarify the obscenity
     statutes. However, attorneys report that little time
     is spent on enforcement of obscenity laws.

365. Wilson, W. Cody, and Sylvia Jacobs. "Pornography and
     Youth: A Survey of Sex Educators and Counselors."
     *Technical Report of the Commission on Obscenity and
     Pornography: Societal Control Mechanisms, vol. V.*
     Washington, D.C.: U.S. Government Printing Office,
     1971, pp. 369-373.

     Members of the American Association of Sex Educators
     and Counselors responded to questionnaires regarding
     their perception of the effects of erotica on adoles-
     cents. Results indicate that youths, male and female,
     had an interest in explicit sexual material, but that
     few members felt consequences of exposure to be harmful.
     A significant number felt such materials give status
     and information, and provide a harmless outlet for sexual
     impulses.

366. Winick, Charles. "Some Observations on Characteristics
     of Patrons of Adult Theaters and Bookstores." *Tech-
     nical Report of the Commission on Obscenity and Por-
     nography: The Marketplace: Empirical Studies, vol. IV.*
     Washington, D.C.: U.S. Government Printing Office,
     1971, pp. 225-244.

     Patrons were observed in terms of dress, behavior,
     age and ethnicity. Patrons of theaters tended to be
     older than those at bookstores, and of a higher economic
     class. Behavior and appearance of customers tended toward
     the conventional, with the environment being more muted
     than in traditional retail concerns.

367. Winick, Charles. "A Study of Consumers of Explicitly
     Sexual Materials: Some Functions Served by Adult Movies."

Technical Report of the Commission on Obscenity and Pornography: The Marketplace: Empirical Studies, vol. IV. Washington, D.C.: U.S. Government Printing Office, 1971, pp. 245-262.

Intensive personal interviews were conducted with 100 patrons of adult movie theaters. Particular attention was paid to the function such movies serve for various patrons. Use patterns, stimulus functions and fantasy aspects were included. Younger patrons perceived educational and informational functions in the films. Authors noted that simplistic "either/or" explanations of the functions of erotic materials are not borne out by the study.

368. Zetterberg, Hans L. "The Consumers of Pornography Where It is Easily Available: The Swedish Experience." *Technical Report of the Commission on Obscenity and Pornography: The Consumer and the Community, vol. IX.* Washington, D.C.: U.S. Government Printing Office, 1971, pp. 453-467.

Interviews, including questionnaire responses, were conducted in Sweden to assess attitudinal and behavioral characteristics related to pornography use. Findings suggested that most consumers of erotica are young males, and consumption increases with higher education. Users tend to be average citizens with satisfactory sex lives. Acceptance of erotica is correlated with rejection of traditional patterns of social control.

369. Zurcher, Louis A., and R. George Kirkpatrick. "Collective Dynamics of Ad Hoc Antipornography Organizations." *Technical Report of the Commission on Obscenity and Pornography: Societal Control Mechanisms, vol. V.* Washington, D.C.: U.S. Government Printing Office, 1971, pp. 83-142.

The natural histories of two ad hoc antipornography organizations were studied employing Smelser's "value-added stages" of collective behavior as an analytical tool. The intensity of the organizations' activity was found to relate directly to the intensity of the value-added stages. Results indicated that such organizations tend to emerge in communities that are under 250,000 population, middle-class and traditional in life style.

370. Zurcher, Louis A., and Robert G. Cushing. "Participants in Ad Hoc Antipornography Organizations: Some Indi-

vidual Characteristics." *Technical Report of the Commission on Obscenity and Pornography: Societal Control Mechanisms, vol. V.* Washington, D.C.: U.S. Government Printing Office, 1971, pp. 143-215.

Basing their work upon an earlier study of the natural history of two antipornography organizations, the authors analyzed the individual characteristics of active participants. Members tended to be middle-aged, raised in small towns, religiously oriented and active, and worked in white-collar occupations or small businesses. Members were also middle-class, married with children, with traditional concepts of marriage and family. Individuals fighting antipornography organizations tended to be better educated, raised in larger cities, less religiously oriented, younger and more liberal.

VII

LEGAL ARTICLES

371. Allain, Alex P. "First and Fourteenth Amendments as
     They Support Libraries, Librarians, Library Systems,
     and Library Development." *Women Lawyers Journal* 60
     (Spring 1974): 55-72.

     Recommends that librarians and the public institutions
     they represent be exempt from criminal obscenity prose-
     cution. The potential effects of *Miller* v. *California*
     on libraries and librarians are examined with regard to
     evaluating collections and acquiring materials. Con-
     cludes that presumption of knowledge is unconstitutional.

372. Bell, Roderick A. "Determining Community Standards."
     ABA Journal 63 (September 1977): 1202-1207.

     Advocates the use of modern, scientific public-opinion
     polls to discover whether a standard exists in a community.
     Jurors cannot be expected to know or represent the views
     of the average citizen in his community. Experts in
     opinion polling must be utilized to define the prevailing
     community standard. The difficulty of statistically
     defining "average" is also discussed.

373. Berbysse, Father Edward J. "Conflict in the Courts: Ob-
     scenity Control and First Amendment Freedoms." *Catholic
     Lawyer* 20 (Winter 1974): 1-29.

     Contends that the freedoms of the First Amendment are
     not absolute and that the regulation of obscenity is per-
     missible under the "police powers" of governments. Danger
     exists not to the freedom of writers and publishers of
     obscenity, but to the public from the "virulent and
     aggressive proliferation of obscenity."

374. Brigman, William E. "The Controversial Role of the Ex-
     pert in Obscenity Litigation." *Capital University Law
     Review* 7 (1978): 519-551.

Examines the difficulties of applying normal law concepts of expert testimony to obscenity trials. Contends
that experts, especially social scientists, are qualified
to testify and explain the concept of community standards.
The special nature of obscenity litigations requires a
lessening of the normal rules of evidence which limit
expert testimony. Experts should be allowed to interpret
and provide guidelines for the jury's deliberation.

375. Bustanante, Luis E., and Forrest W. Lewis. "Pornography,
      the Local Option." *Baylor Law Review* 26 (Winter 1974):
      97-107.

Notes recent Supreme Court cases on obscenity (*Miller*
v. *California*, *Paris Adult Theatre I et al.* v. *Slaton*)
and discusses their effect on earlier decisions such as
Roth v. *United States*. Continued efforts by the Court
to define obscenity have resulted in guidelines: notably,
contemporary community standards, patently offensive sexual conduct and the lack of serious literary value. The
rejection of a national standard will result in some problems, especially in relation to interstate commerce.

376. Byrne, Edward T. "Government Seizures of Imported Ob-
      scene Matter: Section 305 of the Tariff Act of 1930
      and Recent Supreme Court Obscenity Decisions." *Columbia
      Journal of Transnational Law* 13 (1974): 114-142.

Examines the effect the 1973 Supreme Court obscenity
decisions will have on federal attempts to regulate the
importation of obscene materials. The difficulty in
determining which "community standards" to apply is emphasized. Customs officials should have a national
standard, but the Supreme Court has consistently refused
to provide such criteria. The "laxest" community standards could, therefore, be taken as a national standard.

377. Clor, Harry M. "Obscenity and the First Amendment:
      Round Three." *Loyola University of Los Angeles Law
      Review* 7 (June 1974): 207-226.

Contends that the continuing controversy over legal
regulation of obscenity has entered a new phase as a
result of the Supreme Court decisions of June, 1973.
The first phase involved *Roth* v. *United States* and the
second phase centered around *A Book Named "John Cleland's
Memoirs of a Woman of Pleasure"* v. *Attorney General of
Massachusetts*. This new phase results from *Miller* v.
California and associated cases.

378. Clor, Harry M. "Public Morality and Free Expression:
      The Judicial Search for Principles of Reconciliation."
      Hastings Law Journal 28 (July 1977): 1305-1313.

      Reviews recent cases that deal with the power of local
      government to regulate obscenity. If substantial public
      interest can be shown, "secondary regulation" of adult
      theaters and pornographic materials is legal and should
      be allowed. Concludes that First Amendment rights can
      be maintained and community interests protected at the
      same time.

379. "Community Standards, Class Actions, and Obscenity Under
      Miller v. *California*." *Harvard Law Review* 88 (June
      1975): 1838-1874.

      Forecasts the impact *Miller* v. *California* will have on
      future obscenity cases. The guidelines established by
      the court are "overbroad" and may result in the suppres-
      sion of works of serious value, which are supposedly
      protected. Suggests that both class-action procedures
      and federal declaratory judgments can be used to obtain
      judgments of nonobscenity that would apply nationwide.

380. Davidow, R.P., and M.O. Boyle. "Obscenity Laws in
      England and the United States: A Comparative Analysis."
      Nebraska Law Review 56 (1977): 249-288.

      Compares the obscenity laws of England and the United
      States. Similar judicial attitudes, such as viewing the
      problem as one of distinguishing between socially valu-
      able materials and worthless and corrupting publications,
      are presented. Differences are more evident in the pro-
      cedural area, i.e. the procedure for seizure of allegedly
      pornographic materials. The major difference is that in
      England obscenity is not restricted to sex, but can in-
      clude violence or drugs.

381. Davis, T.L. "Defects in Indiana's Pornographic Nuisance
      Act." *Indiana Law Journal* 49 (1974): 320-333.

      Claims the Indiana Pornographic Nuisance Act is prob-
      ably unconstitutional as a result of *Miller* v. *California*.
      The following defects are discussed: (1) inadequate
      safeguards in preliminary injunction proceedings; (2)
      absence of jury involvement; (3) vagueness; (4) prior
      restraint; and (5) a "chilling effect" on the exercise
      of First Amendment rights by theater owners. Concludes
      that a nuisance act is too imprecise a means to control
      obscenity.

382. Edelstein, Stephen J., and Kenneth Mott. "Collateral
      Problems in Obscenity Regulation: A Uniform Approach
      to Prior Restraints, Community Standards, and Judgment
      Preclusion." *Seton Hall Law Review* 7 (Spring 1976):
      543-587.

      Investigates the possibility of using prior restraints,
      judgment preclusion, and contemporary community standards
      in regulating obscenity on the state or federal level.
      Any of these procedures may conflict with First Amend-
      ment rights. Therefore, great care must be taken to
      limit the effects of such actions. Analysis is based
      on the definition of obscenity as stated in *Miller* v.
      California.

383. Eich, William F. "From Ulysses to Portnoy: A Pornography
      Primer." *Marquette Law Review* 53 (Summer 1970): 155-
      171.

      Reviews the uncertainty of the Supreme Court's defini-
      tion of obscenity as demonstrated in their decisions
      from the Roth decision through the 1960s. Obscenity may
      eventually be protected under the First Amendment except
      when it might prove harmful to children or when it amounts
      to unsolicited intrusion on a person's privacy.

384. Fahringer, Herald Price. "The Defense of an Obscenity
      Prosecution." *Trial* 14 (May 1978): 32-34.

      Reviews the rise of obscenity prosecutions and demon-
      strates both the difficulty of proving obscenity and
      the dangers such prosecutions represent to the First
      Amendment. Defines "average person," "contemporary
      community standards" and "prurient interest." Concludes
      that pornographers, representing the "dark side of the
      First Amendment," must be protected if other types of
      expression are to remain free of governmental control.

385. Fahringer, Herald P., and Michael J. Brown. "Rise and
      Fall of Roth--A Critique of the Recent Supreme Court
      Obscenity Decisions." *Criminal Law Bulletin* 10
      (November 1974): 785-826.

      Analyzes numerous recent Supreme Court decisions on
      obscenity. The significance of *Miller* v. *California* is
      emphasized, and its guidelines are compared to those
      established earlier in *Roth* v. *United States*. Contends
      that control of pornography should be left to the "self-
      regulating forces of the public's taste."

386. Fahringer, Herald P., and Paul J. Cambria, Jr. "The
     New Weapons Being Used in Waging War Against Pornog-
     raphy." *Capital University Law Review* 7 (1978): 553-
     578.

     Identifies and discusses various legal procedures used
     to fight pornography: (1) use of zoning laws; (2) use of
     building codes; (3) police harassment; and (4) use of
     nuisance laws. Contends that these "low visibility
     statutes" are ideally suited for prosecuting certain
     types of pornography which are not easily controlled
     by formal obscenity laws. There is, however, high po-
     tential for abuse of these ordinances, especially the
     use of nuisance laws.

387. Falk, Gerhard. "The Roth Decision in the Light of
     Sociological Knowledge." *American Bar Association
     Journal* 54 (March 1968): 288-292.

     The key concepts of "contemporary community standards"
     and the "average" person are discussed from a sociological
     perspective. The conclusion is drawn that little socio-
     logical sense can be made of these terms, and that their
     meaning is arbitrarily defined by authority and not by
     consensus.

388. Fleishman, S. "Mr. Justice Douglas on Sex Censorship."
     Los Angeles Bar Journal 51 (May 1976): 560-562.

     Reviews the opinions of Justice Douglas in numerous
     obscenity cases. The majority of opinions cited are
     dissenting. His first major dissent was in *Roth* v.
     United States (1957). Justice Douglas's dissenting
     opinions in *Ginsberg* v. *New York* and *Miller* v. *California*
     are also discussed and quoted at length.

389. Forkosch, Morris D. "Obscenity, Copyright, and the Arts."
     New England Law Review 10 (Fall 1974): 1-24.

     Contends that works of art, whether visual or nonvisual,
     may have difficulty securing copyrights as a result of
     the obscenity guidelines established by the Supreme
     Court in *Miller* v. *California* (1973). Additional prob-
     lems are seen with regard to postal and customs regula-
     tions. Concerned citizens are urged to fight any further
     censorship of the arts and artists.

390. Forkosch, Morris D. "Pornobscenity, Morals, and Judicial
     Discrimination." *Capital University Law Review* 7
     (1978): 579-619.

Points out the difficulty in distinguishing between
the "nonpornobscene, the soft-core pornobscene, and the
hard-core pornobscene." Contends that the courts, especially the Supreme Court, must keep the power of review. Different kinds of obscenity, i.e. pornographic
materials or shouted obscenities, exist and must be considered separately. Pornobscenity cases do not allow
totally objective decisions, and the subjectivity of the
judges is often evident.

391. Frankel, Charles. "Moral Environment of the Law."
      Minnesota Law Review 61 (June 1977): 921-960.

      Considers the moral and philosophical issues involved
      in the legal enforcement of morality through censorship.
      The relationship of law and legal procedures to higher
      moral principles is also discussed. Concludes that por-
      nography serves an important purpose by being an "escape
      hatch" from the rules and mores of society.

392. Friedman, Jane M. "Zoning 'Adult' Movies: The Potential
      Impact of *Young* v. *American Mini Theaters.*" *Hastings
      Law Journal* 28 (July 1977): 1293-1304.

      Analyzes examples of a new legal concept: "adult" law.
      The use of zoning ordinances to regulate and contain
      "adult" motion picture theaters is discussed. The Su-
      preme Court approved such activity in *Young* v. *American
      Mini Theaters, Inc.* in 1976. The difficulty of defining
      "adult" is emphasized. Concludes that this decision
      creates a "censorial nightmare for the *entire* motion
      picture industry."

393. Friedman, Leon. "The Ginzburg Decision and the Law."
      American Scholar 36 (Winter 1966-1967): 71-91.

      Discussion of the Ginzburg case before the Supreme
      Court in 1966. Decision is viewed in light of other
      cases and particularly the Roth decision, and general
      remarks are made concerning obscenity and pornography
      laws.

394. Gaynor, Michael J. "Obscenity Laws: Après *Stanley*, le
      déluge?" *Catholic Lawyer* 17 (Winter 1971): 45-62.

      Summarizes and analyzes *Stanley* v. *Georgia*, which
      ruled that private possession of obscene material is not
      illegal. Demonstrates that subsequent court decisions
      have been contradictory in interpreting the Stanley
      decision. Concludes that future Supreme Court decisions

will: (1) guarantee the privacy of unwilling adults and the protection of children; and (2) definitely not be unanimous.

395. Gaynor, Michael J. "Obscenity Law: Le Déluge Postponed." *Catholic Lawyer* 17 (Summer 1971): 255-266.

Analyzes two Supreme Court cases, *United States* v. *Thirty-Seven (37) Photographs* and *United States* v. *Reidel*. These decisions represent an attempt by the Court to clarify its decision in *Stanley* v. *Georgia*, which allowed private possession of obscene materials. Obscenity is constitutionally protected, not as free speech, but because of the right to privacy. Its regulation is to be determined by Congress and state legislatures, not the courts.

396. Hardy, John. "*Miller* v. *California* and *Paris Adult Theatre I* v. *Slaton*: The Obscenity Doctrine Reformulated." *Columbia Human Rights Law Review* 6 (Spring 1974): 219-237.

Reviews Supreme Court attempts at dealing with pornography. The 1973 decisions indicate a change from the *de novo* review which had previously been accepted to more state authority in such matters. Concludes this is a "false resolution" to the problem because the central issue of the dual-level concept of speech remains. The Court must eventually distinguish between obscene and protected speech.

397. Hirsch, Richard G., and John L. Ryan. "I Know It When I Seize It: Selected Problems in Obscenity." *Loyola University of Los Angeles Law Review* 4 (February 1971); 9-82.

Focuses on three areas of obscenity law: (1) redeeming social importance; (2) prior judicial determination of obscenity; and (3) Fifth Amendment considerations concerning self-incrimination. For each topic a brief historical summary is presented; then applicable court cases are discussed. Court cases are grouped according to jurisdiction, i.e. the Supreme Court, U.S. District Courts and State Supreme Courts.

398. Hunsaker, David M. "1973 Obscenity-Pornography Decisions: Analysis, Impact, and Legislative Alternatives." *San Diego Law Review* 11 (June 1974): 906-956.

Examines the new standards of obscenity as defined by
the Supreme Court in *Miller* v. *California*. This decision,
while reaffirming the Roth decision, presents a "plural-
istic concept" of obscenity by referring to "contemporary
community standards." Difficulty in applying such standards is emphasized. Alternative models for local and
state legislation are proposed.

399.   Israel, Jerold H., and Rita Ann Burns. "Juvenile Ob-
       scenity Statutes: A Proposal and Analysis." *University
       of Michigan Journal of Law Reform* 9 (Spring 1976):
       413-527.

       Analyzes the various issues involved in drafting a
       juvenile obscenity provision. Statutes adopted by various
       states are summarized. The proposed model statute is
       printed in full and then discussed section by section.
       The statute is based on the New York juvenile obscenity
       statute that was upheld in *Ginsberg* v. *New York* (1968).

400.   Karp, Irwin. "From Roth to Rohauer: Twenty Years of
       Amicus Briefs." *Bulletin of the Copyright Society of
       the U.S.A.* 25 (October 1977): 1-18.

       Reviews the *amicus curiae* briefs filed by the Authors
       League of America beginning in 1959 with *Roth* v. *United
       States* and ending in 1977 with *Rohauer* v. *Killian Shows,
       Inc.* Five types of cases are considered: (1) freedom
       of expression; (2) libel and privacy; (3) contract; (4)
       tax issues; and (5) copyright. Copyright cases repre-
       sented the area of most involvement. Concludes that
       decisions often depend on the particular judges involved
       and that both the First Amendment and the Copyright Act
       will be continually reinterpreted.

401.   Kassner, Herbert S. "Obscenity Leads to Perversion."
       New York Law Forum 20 (Winter 1975): 551-568.

       Warns that as the result of the Supreme Court's 1973
       decisions the United States is entering an era of "thought
       prohibition." Only a change in the composition of the
       Court can reverse the "constitutional perversions" dis-
       played in *Miller* and *Hamling*. Concludes that First
       Amendment issues will now be judged in the trial courts.

402.   Kim, Chin. "Constitution and Obscenity: Japan and the
       U.S.A." *American Journal of Comparative Law* 23
       (Spring 1975): 255-283.

Compares Japanese and American obscenity decisions. Cultural differences, as well as constitutional provisions, have resulted in somewhat different approaches to obscenity. In Japan a definite trend toward censorship is evident, but in the United States the opposite has been true.

403. Leventhal, Harold. "The 1973 Round of Obscenity-Pornography Decisions." *ABA Journal* 59 (November 1973): 1261-1266.

Reviews the guidelines for dealing with obscenity and pornography established by the Supreme Court in *Miller* v. *California*. These "concrete guidelines" may apply to past problems, but new and different problems are forecast. The inappropriateness of criminal and judicial involvement with the subjective problems of art and morality is stressed.

404. Lockhart, William B. "Escape from the Chill of Uncertainty: Explicit Sex and the First Amendment." *Georgia Law Review* 9 (Spring 1975): 533-587.

Reviews the effect of the *Miller* v. *California* decision by the Supreme Court. Contends that the guidelines prescribed are too broad and that this inherent vagueness has resulted in a "chilling effect" on the production of any material that might possibly be labeled obscene, including serious literary works.

405. Loewy, Arnold H. "A Better Test for Obscenity: Better for the Libertarians." *Hastings Law Journal* 28 (July 1977): 1315-1323.

Examines briefly several Supreme Court cases which deal with the conflict between First Amendment rights and governmental interests. Argues that no regulation whose purpose is to prevent access to sexually explicit material is constitutional. However, a regulation that deals with an accepted area of state concern, such as public health, but which does not deny access, is constitutional and should be used in regulating obscenity.

406. Loewy, Arnold H. "A New Test for Obscenity." *Trial* 14 (May 1978): 35-37.

Investigates the reasons given for legislative attempts to control pornography. Reports reaction to test for obscenity proposed earlier by the author. Contends that any legislation designed solely to limit access by adults

to pornography is illegal, but that any regulation controlling such publications which does not restrict access is constitutional. Statutes should focus on the
harm caused by adult establishments, not on whether a
particular book or film is obscene.

407. Marcin, Raymond B. "Ideological Pluralism and Govern-
      ment Regulation of Private Morality." *Capital Univer-
      sity Law Review* 7 (1978): 621-630.

      Discusses the legal ability and the moral right of the
      state to legislate morality. Contends the state has
      both the power and the right to regulate public acts of
      immorality, but neither the moral right to control nor
      an effective means of controlling private behavior.
      Details the problem in American society of determining
      what justice is and then justifying it to all citizens.

408. Mayer, M.F. "New Approach to Obscenity--the Conspiracy
      Doctrine." *St. Louis University Law Journal* 21 (1977):
      366-373.

      Criticizes the use of the conspiracy approach to ob-
      scenity prosecutions. The conspiracy doctrine is vague,
      allows for easy venue manipulations and presents diffi-
      culties in determining point of withdrawal from the con-
      spiracy. This federal conspiracy statute was used to
      obtain a conviction of actor Harry Reems for his partici-
      pation in *Deep Throat*. Urges a reevaluation of the entire
      conspiracy doctrine.

409. Medina, D. Rangel. "Mexican Law on Obscenity." *Lawyer
      of the Americas* 7 (June 1975): 337-348.

      Reviews Mexican legal provisions for dealing with ob-
      scenity. Articles and sections of the law are quoted
      and then analyzed with reference to judicial decisions.
      A 1971 decision declaring *Playboy* illegal is examined
      in detail. Concludes the concept of obscenity is "im-
      precise, ambiguous, and undefinable."

410. Milligan, William W. "Obscenity: Malum in se or Only
      in Context? The Supreme Court's Long Ordeal."
      Capital University Law Review 7 (1978): 631-645.

      Argues that obscenity can best be classified as a
      public nuisance. Obscenity, like other public nuisances,
      should be made a strict liability offense, not a criminal
      prosecution. Fines, not imprisonment, are meaningful
      and appropriate penalties. Concludes that acceptance

of the public nuisance theory would relieve the Supreme
Court of direct responsibility for determining and controlling pornography.

411. Neef, Marian, and Stuart Nagel. "Judicial Behavior in
Pornography Cases." *Journal of Urban Law* 52 (1974):
1-23.

Reviews attempts by the Supreme Court to suggest
guidelines for lower courts to follow concerning the control of or access to various types of pornographic materials. Results of a quantitative study indicate that
certain factors seem not likely to affect judicial decisions in pornography cases: (1) intent of the violator
to sell rather than simply possess; (2) method of distribution used; (3) reputation of the author; and (4) reputation of the publisher.

411a. Payton, J.M. "Child Pornography Legislation." *Journal
of Family Law* 17 (1979): 505-543.

Reviews laws on child pornography in the United States.
Analyzes the federal laws, especially the Protection of
Children Against Sexual Exploitation Act of 1977, and de-
tails the great increase in state legislation since
1977. Federal courts have determined that both federal
and state laws must comply with the Supreme Court's
guidelines on obscenity.

412. Rendleman, Doug. "Civilizing Pornography: The Case for
an Exclusive Obscenity Nuisance Statute." *University
of Chicago Law Review* 44 (Spring 1977): 509-560.

Argues that criminal penalties are too severe and ineffective in regulating obscenity. An exclusive civil
sanction utilizing injunctions is proposed to replace
criminal obscenity laws. A comprehensive nuisance
statute is presented that would allow a judge to issue
an injunction regulating obscenity. This might result
in more equitable regulation of pornography.

413. Reynolds, Richard R. "Our Misplaced Reliance on Early
Obscenity Cases." *ABA Journal* 61 (February 1975):
220-222.

Examines 17th- and 18th-century English obscenity
cases and points out that they were primarily political
prosecutions. Obscenity itself was not viewed as a
serious matter. Warns against referring to these early
cases as possible precedents for censorship.

414. Rogge, O. John. "The Obscenity Terms of the Court."
      Villanova Law Review 17 (February 1972): 393-462.

      Reviews the obscenity cases decided by the Supreme
      Court in its 1970-1971 term. The great number of cases
      has resulted in the Court's becoming the "High Court of
      the Obscenity." Suggests that obscenity must be taken
      out of the Supreme Court. Concludes that consenting
      adults have a due process right to obtain and view any
      type of material and that obscenity legislation should
      be limited to protecting children and nonconsenting
      adults.

415. Rosenblum, Robert. "The Judicial Politics of Obscenity."
      Pepperdine Law Review 3 (Winter 1975): 1-25.

      Argues that current judicial policy regarding obscenity
      is "untenable" and urges that the Supreme Court either
      avoid the issue entirely or revert to the policy it had
      established during the period 1967 to 1971. The con-
      tinued split among the Supreme Court justices has re-
      sulted in conflicting opinions among state courts. This
      produces more cases to be decided by the Supreme Court.

416. Samek, R.A. "Pornography as a Species of Second-Order
      Sexual Behavior: A Submission for Law Reform."
      Dalhousie Law Journal 1 (December 1973): 265-293.

      Distinguishes between overt sexual behavior, whether
      physical or imaginary, and any behavior that stimulates
      some form of overt sexual behavior. The latter is termed
      second-order sexual behavior and is the most objection-
      able because it results in commercial exploitation of
      sex. It includes producing pornography and operating
      pornographic theaters. However, second-order sexual
      behavior is controllable through administrative, not
      criminal, means. If the profitability of second-order
      sexual behavior is diminished, the problem of first-order
      pornography will also be lessened.

417. Schauer, Frederick F. "Reflections on 'Contemporary
      Community Standards': The Perpetuation of an Irrelevant
      Concept in the Law of Obscenity." *North Carolina Law
      Review* 56 (January 1978): 1-28.

      Argues that the concept of contemporary community
      standards as presented in *Miller* v. *California* (1973)
      is "anachronistic and useless" in determining obscenity.
      The concept lacks historical and precedential justifica-
      tion, and it also serves no independent purpose in apply-

ing the other tests of obscenity suggested by *Miller*.
Eliminating the contemporary community standard would
result in more consistent application of local obscenity
standards.

418. Schauer, Frederick F. "The Return of Variable Obscenity."
      Hastings Law Journal 28 (July 1977): 1275-1291.

      Explores the possible effects of a return to the con-
      cept of variable obscenity as opposed to a strict defi-
      nitional approach to obscenity. The decision in *Young*
      v. *American Mini Theaters, Inc.* allows zoning restric-
      tions on sexually explicit materials and, consequently,
      seems to indicate a change in the Court's approach to
      defining obscenity. The history of the variable ob-
      scenity approach is given and the conclusion is that
      the constant approach should be maintained.

418a. Schauer, Frederick. "Speech and 'Speech'--Obscenity and
      'Obscenity': An Exercise in the Interpretation of Con-
      stitutional Language." *Georgetown Law Journal* 67
      (April 1979): 899-933.

      Responds to criticism of the Supreme Court's use of
      the "two-level" theory of speech whereby obscenity is
      judged not to be a type of speech protected by the First
      Amendment. Concludes that obscenity which functions
      primarily as a surrogate sexual act and lacks any com-
      municative intent is not properly considered "speech."
      Therefore, the Court's rulings which attempt to isolate
      such material are not only correct, but also may actually
      work to strengthen the First Amendment.

419. Schneder, Dan W. "Authority of the Register of Copyrights
      to Deny Registration of a Claim to Copyright on the
      Ground of Obscenity." *Chicago-Kent Law Review* 51
      (1975): 691-724.

      Argues that the Register of Copyrights does not have
      the authority to deny copyright because of alleged ob-
      scenity. No direct legal support for such authority is
      found in either statutes or case law. Concludes that
      considering the Copyright Office as a federal censor
      would be "ill-advised." Administrative and constitu-
      tional limitations on such authority are presented, and
      the courtroom is recommended as the only appropriate
      authority in such matters.

420. Shugrue, Richard E., and Patricia Zieg. "Atlas for Ob-
      scenity: Exploring Community Standards." *Creighton
      Law Review* 7 (Spring 1974): 157-181.

Indicates that the Supreme Court has consistently
failed to adequately define obscenity. The guidelines
established by *Miller* v. *California* fail to define
specifically the community's standards that are to be
considered and, consequently, have been interpreted in
a variety of ways by lower courts. Urges the use of
expert testimony to establish community standards.

421. Stanmeyer, William A. "Obscene Evils v. Obscure Truths:
      Some Notes of First Principles." *Capital University
      Law Review* 7 (1978): 647-682.

Discusses six elements of the debate on pornography:
(1) freedom of speech protection; (2) the definition of
pornography; (3) the harm of pornography; (4) the need
for virtue in a free society; (5) the educative role of
law; and (6) parental rights to educate to decency. Contends that a free society may, and should, use the law
to regulate extreme forms of pornography.

422. Teachout, Peter R. "Chains of Tradition, Instruments
      of Freedom, Contours of the Emerging Right to Community
      in Obscenity Law." *Capital University Law Review* 7
      (1970): 683-731.

Urges the Supreme Court to abandon the two-level approach to obscenity. Cites failures and abuses of obscenity guidelines and legislation. Obscenity should
be protected under the First Amendment, but the state
and local communities should be given broader control
over commercial pornography within their jurisdictions.
Advocates the use of zoning ordinances not only to
regulate pornography establishments, but also to zone
them out of particular locations.

423. Tushnet, Mark. "Technical and Economic Aspects of the
      Production of Sexually Explicit Materials." *Capital
      University Law Review* 7 (1978): 733-746.

Argues that the Supreme Court decisions in June, 1973,
did not solve the problem of obscenity litigation. The
two-tiered theory of freedom of speech, where some types
of speech are totally protected and others totally un-
protected, is not workable. Pornography can be legally
controlled by direct regulation of content or regulation
of production and marketing. The former is often im-
possible, but the latter, although currently favored by
the Supreme Court, raises other legal questions.

VIII

COURT CASES

424. *A Book Named "John Cleland's Memoirs of a Woman of Pleasure"* v. *Attorney General of Massachusetts* 383 U.S. 413 (1966).

In this case, known as the *Fanny Hill* case, the court explicitly stated the tripartite test for obscenity. It must be established that "a) the dominant theme of the material taken as a whole appeals to a prurient interest in sex; b) the material is patently offensive because it affronts contemporary community standards relating to the description or representation of sexual matters; and c) the material is utterly without redeeming social value." (See items 212, 273, 293, 377, 435.)

425. *Butler* v. *Michigan* 352 U.S. 380 (1957).

Rules on the issue of obscenity statutes which restrict materials that tend to corrupt youths even when the materials are being used by adults. Court argued that to restrict materials merely because they might corrupt a youth "is to reduce the adult population of Michigan to reading only what is fit for children." Thus, the statute curtails the rights given in the Due Process Clause of the Fourteenth Amendment.

426. *Ginsberg* v. *New York* 390 U.S. 629 (1968).

Argues that obscenity statutes which restrict minors' access to obscene materials do not unconstitutionally restrict the minors' right to freedom of expression. Argues the state has an interest in protecting parents' rights to guide their children, and also claims an independent interest in their well-being. (See items 388, 399.)

427. *Ginzburg* v. *United States* 383 U.S. 463 (1966).

Concerns primarily the issue of whether material not
wholly obscene in itself can be considered obscene in
the context of the setting promoting the material.
Majority argued that "pandering" such material by promoting those aspects which would appeal to the prurient
interest may serve to determine the work as obscene.
(See items 33, 52, 212, 393.)

428. *Hamling* v. *United States* 418 U.S. 87 (1974).

In this case, involving dissemination of sexually explicit materials through the mails, the Court dealt
with the issue of applying the Miller decision to convictions occurring before the decision but appealed
after. Court upheld the applicability of Miller. (See
items 166, 401.)

429. *Jacobellis* v. *Ohio* 378 U.S. 184 (1964).

Based on the conviction of a theater owner who exhibited a film, *The Lovers*, consequently found to be
obscene. Affirms a three-point test for obscenity,
i.e. that the material (1) appeals to the prurient
interest; (2) is patently offensive; and (3) is utterly
without redeeming social importance. Also indicated
that the constitutional status of obscene material must
be based on a national rather than local standard. (See
items 33, 293.)

430. *Jenkins* v. *Georgia* 199 S.E. 2d 183 (1964).

Involves the conviction of Billy Jenkins for exhibit-
ing the film *Carnal Knowledge* in Georgia. Argues that
states have legitimate interest in regulating obscene
materials and that *Carnal Knowledge* conforms to the
definition of obscenity in the Alabama code. (See items
166, 200.)

431. *Manual Enterprises* v. *Day* 370 U.S. 478 (1962).

Based on a case in which the U.S. Post Office barred
magazines considered obscene. The Court supplemented
the Roth decision by adding that the material must
possess the element of "patent offensiveness."

432. *Miller* v. *California* 413 U.S. 15 (1973).

Rejected the test that obscenity must be "utterly
without redeeming social value." Established the follow-

ing guidelines: (1) whether the average person, applying contemporary community standards, would find that
the work, taken as a whole, appeals to the prurient
interest; (2) whether the work depicts or describes, in
a patently offensive way, sexual conduct specifically
defined by the applicable state law; and (3) whether
the work, taken as whole, lacks serious literary, artistic, political or scientific value. Court also noted
that "community standards" are distinct from national
standards and that juries can consider the materials
in light of local standards. (See items 155, 166, 167,
200, 258, 263, 278, 371, 375, 377, 379, 385, 389, 396,
398, 401, 403, 404, 417, 420, 428.)

433. *Mishkin* v. *New York* 383 U.S. 502 (1966).

Primarily concerned with depictions of bondage or
sadomasochism. Court rejected the claim that the "average
person" criterion was not satisfied and argued that
when material is aimed at a particular group, the Roth
criterion is satisfied if the "material taken as a whole
appeals to the prurient interest in sex of the members
of that group." (See item 33.)

434. *Paris Adult Theatre I et al.* v. *Slaton* 413 U.S. 49 (1973).

Concerns the showing of two films in a Georgia theater
which exhibited the films to consenting adults only.
Court argued that the states have a legitimate interest
in regulating obscene materials to protect the "quality
of life and the total community environment," and that
adult theaters are not excluded from the states' regulatory function in this area. (See items 375, 396.)

435. *Redrup* v. *New York* 386 U.S. 767 (1967).

In case based on the sale of two paperback books from
a New York City newsstand, Court indicated lack of una-
nimity in defining obscenity, though tripartite criterion
established in *Memoirs* was restated. Court concluded
that no issue of privacy, harm to juveniles or pandering
arose. (See items 212, 293.)

436. *Regina* v. *Hicklin* L.R. 3 Q.B. (1868).

Based on the distribution of an anti-Roman Catholic
pamphlet. Case took place in the Court of Queens Bench
in England. Provided an early formulation for the
definition of obscene, which according to Chief Justice
Cockburn was: "whether the tendency of the matter charged

as obscenity is to deprave and corrupt those whose minds
are open to such immoral influences, and into whose hands
a publication of this sort may fall." This decision,
promulgated in the Victorian era, was the primary regula-
tor of obscenity in the courts until well into the
20th century. (See item 293.)

437. *Roth* v. *United States* 354 U.S. 476 (1957).

Case involved the conviction of two individuals con-
ducting business in the sale and distribution of pornographic materials. Majority of the Court held that obscenity "is not within the area of constitutionally
protected speech or press." Affirmed the following test
of obscenity: "whether to the average person, applying
contemporary community standards, the dominant theme of
the material taken as a whole appeals to the prurient
interest." Also argued that obscenity is "utterly without redeeming social importance." (See items 30, 33,
54, 141, 182, 212, 228, 243, 248, 267, 293, 375, 383,
385, 387, 388, 393.)

438. *Smith* v. *California* 361 U.S. 147 (1959).

Dealt with the question of whether an individual
proprietor of a bookstore can be subjected to criminal
penalties under obscenity statutes if he is unaware of
the contents of the material deemed to be obscene. Court
asserted that conviction would have chilling effect on
bookstore operators and violate constitutional protections
of speech and expression. (See item 245.)

439. *Splawn* v. *California* 431 U.S. 595 (1977).

Deals primarily with the Court's affirmation of pandering as sufficient grounds for conviction and the use of
statutes enacted after the offense for the purpose of
instructing the jury regarding sufficient grounds to
convict for pandering. (See item 245.)

440. *Stanley* v. *Georgia* 394 U.S. 557 (1969).

Based on the discovery of two obscene films in a home
which was being searched for evidence of another crime.
Court ruled that "mere private possession of obscene
matter cannot constitutionally be made a crime." Court
also noted that lack of ideological content in the films
or in materials in general is not a relevant considera-
tion. (See items 180, 273, 293, 294, 394, 395.)

441. *United States* v. *Reidel* 402 U.S. 351 (1971).

      Involves the mailing of obscene materials. Court
      ruled that the right to view pornography in one's home
      affirmed in *Stanley* v. *Georgia* does not protect the in-
      dividual using the mails to distribute such materials.
      (See item 395.)

442. *United States* v. *31 Photographs*. 156 F. Supp. 350
      (1957).

      Deals with importing sexually explicit materials for
      the purpose of research. Court ruled that the material
      does not meet the criterion for obscenity because the
      term "average person" applies in this case to the re-
      searchers, who were not likely to experience an arousal
      of their prurient interest. (See item 178.)

443. *United States* v. *Thirty-Seven (37) Photographs* 402 U.S.
      363 (1971).

      Two adult theaters in Georgia were enjoined from show-
      ing two films declared to be obscene, though the films
      were ostensibly restricted to adults only. Court ruled
      that such a restriction does not remove the state's
      power to regulate such materials. Court further noted
      that although there is no scientific evidence supporting
      the argument that pornography is harmful, the state may
      determine that it is and act to protect its citizenry.
      (See item 395.)

444. *Young* v. *American Mini Theaters, Inc*. 427 U.S. 50
      (1976).

      Based on the issue of whether zoning laws may regulate
      commercial enterprises such as adult theaters. Court
      held that zoning regulations in such cases are not vio-
      lations of First Amendment protections against prior
      restraint. (See items 128, 392, 418.)

PERIODICALS CITED

AUTHOR INDEX

Abelson, Herbert I., 111,
   290
Allain, Alex P., 371
Allen, Gina, 255
Allen, Walter, 3a
Alpert, Hollis, 23
Alschuler, Martha, 291
Amoroso, Donald M., 61, 62,
   64, 65, 108, 292
Anchell, Melvin, 350, 354
Anderson, Joan, 123
Andrist, Ralph K., 226
Asher, Thomas R., 349
Athanasiou, Robert, 63, 162

Bachy, Victor, 113
Bahm, Robert M., 1
Barber, D.F., 2
Barnett, Lewis D., 363
Barnett, Walter, 114
Baron, Robert A., 63a, 63b,
   63c
Barrett, Gary, 71b
Barrett, James K., 227
Bauman, Richard, 346
Beeson, Trevor, 196
Bell, Paul A., 63c
Bell, Robert R., 76
Bell, Roderick A., 372
Bender, Paul, 228, 293, 294
Benson, C. Neil, 354
Ben-Veniste, Richard, 295
Berbysse, Father Edward J.,
   373
Berger, Alan S., 115, 296,
   297

Berns, Walter, 116
Bickel, Alexander, 117
Birkelbach, Ronald D., 118
Blake, Richard A., 229
Blount, Winton M., 230
Bonfield, Arthur E., 119
Bonniwell, Bernard L., 120,
   350
Bosmajian, Haig A., 3, 121
Bovras, James, 122
Bowman, Charles K., 193, 194
Boyle, M.O., 380
Braucht, G. Nicholas, 71,
   309, 310
Bretnor, Reginald, 231
Bridge, Peter, 232
Brigman, William E., 374
Brock, Timothy C., 134, 298
Bromberger, Bryan, 299, 300
Brothers, Joyce, 233
Brown, Coke, 123
Brown, Marvin, 61, 62, 63d,
   64, 65, 108, 292,
Brown, Michael J., 385
Brown, Sharon, 164
Buckley, Tom, 234
Burgess, Anthony, 27
Burggraf, Linda, 123
Burns, Rita A., 399
Burt, Mary E. Hamilton, 124
Bustanante, Luis E., 375
Byrne, Donn, 66, 67, 301
Byrne, Edward J., 376

Cahill, Marriane E., 354
Calderone, Mary S., 125

SUBJECT INDEX

Acid phosphatase secretion, 320
Adolescents, 115, 296, 297, 311, 342, 365
Adult bookstores, 145, 163, 312, 337, 435
"Adult" law, 392
Adult movie theaters. *See* Films
Adult paperbacks, 175
Aesthetics, 38, 39a, 42, 116, 198, 207, 217
Age and pornography, 59, 91, 95, 112, 189, 361, 363, 365, 425, 426
Age restrictions. *See* Age and pornography
Aggression and pornography, 63a, 63b, 63c, 71a, 71b, 71c, 82a, 90a, 91a, 110a, 112a, 112b, 336, 347
American Association of Sex Educators and Counselors, 365
American Tragedy, An, 35
Anticensorship. *See* Censorship, anti
Antipornography, 7, 9, 10, 15, 24, 39, 58, 60, 113, 143
Antipornography organizations, 31, 51, 118, 148, 149, 192, 193, 194, 195, 259, 284, 369, 370

Antisocial behavior. *See* Crime
Arcades, 163, 181, 337
Argentina, 343
Aristotle's *Poetics*, 222
Arousal responses, 37, 61, 63, 63a, 63b, 63c, 63d, 64, 68, 71a, 71b, 71c, 71d, 72, 72a, 73, 82, 82a, 90a, 91a, 93, 98, 100, 101, 104, 110a, 112a, 301, 310, 320, 335. *See also* Female arousal
Art, works of. *See* Aesthetics
Attitudes toward pornography 56, 66, 81, 83, 110, 111, 164, 185, 328, 368
Australia, 9, 127, 299
Authors League of America, 400
Availability of pornography, 290, 295, 296, 297, 298, 311, 317, 326, 329, 331. *See also* Business aspects of pornography
Average person, 49, 387, 433, 437, 442

Bibliography, 89, 124, 162. 325
Bickel, Alexander M., 238
Blacks, 150, 309, 317. *See also* Race; Racial stereotypes
Blair, Linda, 244
Book Named "John Cleland's Memoirs of a Woman of Pleasure" v. Attorney

ATE DUE